Stories to Feed Your Soul

Annette Smith

HARVEST HOUSE PUBLISHERS
Eugene, Oregon 97402

Cover by Left Coast Design, Portland, Oregon

Cover illustration copyright © Deb Strain and licensed by Mosaic Licensing, Inc.

STORIES TO FEED YOUR SOUL

Copyright © 1999 by Annette Smith
Published by Harvest House Publishers
Eugene, Oregon 97402

Library of Congress Cataloging-in-Publication Data

Smith, Annette Gail, 1959–
    [Sweeter than honey]
    Stories to feed your soul / Annette Smith.
        p.   cm.
    Originally published: Sweeter than honey. Eugene, OR: Harvest House Publishers, ©1999.
    ISBN 0-7369-0470-0
    1. Christian life—Anecdotes.   I. Title.
BV4517.S63   2001
277.3'0829—dc21   00-047120
                                                                              CIP

Printed in the United States of America

01 02 03 04 / BP / 10 9 8 7 6 5 4 3 2 1

For Russell and Rachel

They are more precious than gold,
than much pure gold;
they are sweeter than honey,
than honey from the comb.
PSALM 19:10

Acknowledgments

During the months I spent writing this book, some extra sweet "honeys" nourished my soul with love, encouragement, confidence, and affection. Warmest thanks to:

- My husband, Randy, and my children,
  Russell and Rachel

- My parents, Louie and Marolyn Woodall

- Friends and personal cheerleaders:
  Jeanna Lambert, Sheri Harrison, Toni Price,
  Stacy Gaylord, and Becky Freeman

- The good folks at Harvest House,
  especially friend and editor Chip MacGregor

To God be the glory.

Contents

ℒ♥ ℒ♥ ℒ♥

Part Four: Time to Play

Sweet Surprises

couple of slices of bread will fill you up, boost your energy, and stop your stomach from growling. Full of calories and carbohydrates, bread will do the job. But as meals go, plain bread is not very tasty. Not much to get excited about. However, if to that slice of bland and boring bread someone adds a swirl of honey, a spoonful of jam, even a sprinkling of sugar—well, now you've got a snack worth eating. Still the same slice of bread; it's the touch of added sweetness that has made the difference.

The stories in this book (most of them fact, some of them with a bit of embellishment) are about those unexpected moments when we open life's lunch sack expecting to find plain bread. We take out a slice and spread out our napkin and prepare to eat. Dutifully (perhaps with a sigh), because we are grateful, we offer up thanks that we have bread.

At least we think we will eat bread for lunch. It looks like plain bread. Smells like it too. Even has a crust. But then we take a bite, and draw back in wonder. Not what we expected. This tastes great! When we weren't looking, someone raided our lunch sacks and replaced our plain, dry bread with delicious butter and honey sandwiches.

Life is full of sweet surprises. Goodness, joy, and meaning pop up unexpectedly in the simplest of circumstances, among the most mundane of details, amid the ho-hum activities of busy life. Special moments, glimpses of the extraordinary, most often come not accompanied by great noise and fanfare, but sandwiched in between all the day-to-day stuff that we do.

In reading the stories held between these pages, tales of ordinary folks living ordinary lives, my hope is that you will recognize and remember times in life when, expecting plain bread, you too tasted honey.

When you do, be sure to thank the One who packed your lunch.

How sweet are your words to my taste,
Sweeter than honey to my mouth!
PSALM 119:103 NKJV

PART ONE

Friends Indeed

CHAPTER ONE

Four Sons, One Potty

While many of our friends married at about the same young age that Randy and I did, most of them chose to delay childbearing for a few years. Before plunging into parenthood, the young couples we knew spoke of goals like Finishing School, Saving for a House, even simply Getting Started.

Not my husband and I. After listening to our friends' flimsy excuses, we shook our heads in wonder and got ourselves pregnant!

Or something like that.

We had been married a mere twenty months when our son, Russell, was born. Since we loved to show him off and assumed he was always welcome, we hauled him and his diaper bag with us everywhere we went. He was passed around, played with, and admired at parties and gatherings. Only when we joined other couples for Sunday night suppers at our friends Lynn and Sam's house did Russell have to compete with a Cocker Spaniel puppy for everyone's attention.

Russell was also the first grandchild born on either side of the family. Two sets of prospective grandparents showed up at the hospital for his birth, sat in the waiting room, and, I'm told, behaved nicely. Upon first sight of Russell, both grand-mothers, I suspect, heaved great silent sighs of relief, thankful that the first grandchild took after *their* side of the family.

Prior to the day I gave birth, my dad had stayed gruffly ambivalent about becoming a father-in-law. But once he held newborn Russell (and admitted that Randy had indeed had *a little* to do with bringing him about), Dad decided that per-haps his new son-in-law possessed a few good qualities after all.

The very month Russell turned one year old, we moved to a university town and into a tiny upstairs apartment so Randy could return to school. And though we were sad to leave behind our old friends, we quickly made new ones. Lots of young couples of every nationality lived in the married stu-dent housing complex where we resided. No one had much money and everyone shared the same laundry room, the same frequently backed-up sewer system, and the same ridicu-lously low rent.

We had a lot in common.

Randy and I quickly made friends with several couples, but found ourselves especially drawn to newlyweds Gwen and Tommy. We first met them at church, then learned they lived in our apartment complex. Gwen was dark-haired and pretty, Tommy tall and lanky. When the two of them drooled over Russell, Randy and I immediately liked them.

Russell, an easy-going toddler, took to most everyone in our circle. However, it was Tommy whom he *really* liked, Tommy whom he wanted to hold him in church, and Tommy to whom he gave sticky kisses and squeeze-around-the-neck hugs. Russell was crazy about Tommy.

And Tommy loved Russell. He played with him, tickled him, talked to him, and read stories to him. There was only one small problem . . . at least everyone except Tommy thought it was a small problem. Russell, unable to pronounce *Tommy,* called his friend, most unfortunately, *Potty*. This tiny mispronunciation greatly distressed the easily embarrassed Tommy.

So, eager to improve our son's verbal skills, certain he could accomplish the task, Tommy would hold Russell on his lap and patiently practice pronunciation with him. "Taahmee," he would say slowly. "Taah-mee. Tommy."

And Russell would sit very still, look into Tommy's face and solemnly repeat, "Paah-tee. Paah-tee. Potty, Potty, Potty."

Especially painful to Tommy were the times when Russell would spot him in public, perhaps at Wal-Mart where we shopped for diapers or at the Piggly-Wiggly where we bought groceries. Russell would sight his friend from *way* across the store, wriggle with excitement, and then point and yell, "Potty, Mommy, POTTY!"

Russell never understood why his friend Potty would duck the other way.

Even though they were still in school, Tommy and Gwen were thrilled when they learned that they too were to have a son. All went well and Gwen's pregnancy blossomed uneventfully. On the morning her water broke, Gwen called Tommy first and me second. Arriving at her door in 30 seconds flat, I talked to her and calmed her and trailed her from room to room mopping up puddles, urging her to *please sit down and wait for Tommy!*

When their baby son was born, Gwen and Tommy named him Caleb. Shortly after his birth, both Tommy and Randy graduated and our families moved on to real jobs and real houses. But we kept in touch.

Over the years, our families have grown. We added a daughter, Rachel, to our number, and Gwen and Tommy went on to have three more healthy boys: Adam, Luke, and Andrew. Randy and I watched as our friends grew to become patient, loving parents.

One spring Sunday afternoon, I stopped in to see Gwen and Tommy. She and I sat in lawn chairs, soaking up some sunshine, sipping iced tea, and enjoying a leisurely chat. Tommy had spent the day working in the yard, was about finished, and had it looking nice. All four little boys played nearby.

"I need to move the van to the street so I can sweep the driveway," Tommy told Gwen. "Watch the kids while I back out, okay?"

"Sure." She yelled for her boys to stay on the grass. Tommy started toward the van.

"Wait Daddy. I wanna go," spoke Caleb.

"Me too," added Adam.

"Guys, I'm not going anywhere," Tommy explained. "I'm just moving the van so I can sweep the driveway."

"But I *really* wanna go, Daddy," implored Caleb.

"Me go too," begged toddler Luke.

"I'm *just* moving the van. I'm not going anywhere."

Baby Andrew, captive in his walker, held up his arms to Tommy and began to wail.

"Andrew wants to go too, Daddy. We *all* want to go." Caleb made the case for the four of them.

Tommy looked at Gwen helplessly.

"Let 'em go. What will it hurt?" she suggested.

"Okay," he shrugged. "Everybody in. But we're *not* going anywhere. I'm just moving the van. Everybody understand?"

"Uh huh."

"Okay, everybody in."

"Wait Daddy, I have to go to the bathroom," announced Luke. He was proud of, but a bit insecure about, his newfound toilet training.

"I need to go too!" It was Adam this time.

Tommy's head dropped. "Okay. Go to the bathroom. Both of you. I'll wait."

Finally, all four boys were ready. Even baby Andrew gurgled triumphantly in Tommy's arms. "Guys," Tommy told them again. "Now we are not going *anywhere*. I'm just moving the van so that I can sweep the sidewalk. Remember?"

The three older boys nodded their complete understanding.

Gwen and I looked at each other. We knew better. The boy's faces were smug. They were thrilled because they were going somewhere. With Daddy.

In the van, Tommy put the key in the ignition.

"Wait Daddy, we're not buckled up!"

"It's alright not to buckle up this time," he assured them. "We're not going anywhere."

"But Daddy, Mama says we *always* have to buckle up," protested Caleb.

"*Always*," echoed Adam and Luke.

Knowing better than to argue with Mommy, Tommy buckled three seat belts and fastened one car seat, slid into the driver's seat and put the van in gear.

"Daddy?"

"Yes, Luke."

"You're not buckled up."

Gwen and I sat in our chairs, held our splitting sides, and sputtered with laughter as we watched Tommy buckle up. Finally, he backed the van thirty feet.

❧ ❧

Russell will graduate from high school this spring. Tommy and Gwen have watched as he's grown and developed and even learned to pronounce his T's. Something about having four sons causes a man to lose all sense of decorum. Since he's become a dad, I can think of little that could rattle or embarrass Tommy, not even being called a bathroom word in Wal-Mart.

He's learned that there is really not much one needs to worry about when it comes to parenting. It's best to relax and enjoy the ride. Only a few rules are worth remembering:

Everybody will *always* want to go.
Somebody will need to go to the bathroom.
Buckle up.
The ride is shorter than you think.

> *Like arrows in the hands of a warrior*
> *Are sons born in one's youth.*
> *Blessed is the man*
> *Whose quiver is full of them.*
> Psalm 127:4,5

CHAPTER TWO

Joseph's Crowning Glory

Most parents who are expecting a second child—parents who already have a little boy—will when pressed, reluctantly, shyly, admit that *yes, we do hope this one's a girl.*

Not Danny and Patti.

Most expectant couples look for their baby to be born handsome or pretty, graceful or athletic.

Not Danny and Patti.

And most young parents, *especially* those anticipating the arrival of a *second* child, *really* hope the newborn will come into the world possessing an easy temperament—what the old wives term a *good baby.*

Not Danny and Patti.

So what *did* Danny and Patti wish for in this, their second and probably last, child?

Hair. Lots of hair.

Danny and Patti's son, Anthony, was not even a year old. Though they'd hoped to have more children, they had not exactly planned on having another baby so soon.

At first Patti attributed her fatigue to simple exhaustion. After all, she *was* thirty-four years old . . . not exactly ancient, but a bit older than most new mothers. Anthony was a busy, active child and a poor sleeper besides. Taking care of him, the house and the yard and the laundry, getting ready for the holidays, helping out with projects at church—all that was enough to make anyone tired, wasn't it?

Sure it was.

But then came the nausea. And when Patti lost her breakfast the fourth morning in a row, and when it did *not* seem to be the stomach flu or a virus, she did what any young woman in her position would do.

"Mother," she spoke into the phone, "you don't think I could be . . . do you?"

She was.

This second time around, Patti knew the prenatal routine well: Answer some questions, get on the scales, give a little blood, and march down the hall to fill up the cup. Finally, up in the stirrups, take a deep breath and without fail, hear the words, *Mrs. DiLoreto, please scoot a little further down to the end of the table.*

No problem.

During this part of the exam, Patti stared at the ceiling and, like most women do, pretended to be in France. Or Australia. Or at least in Dallas.

It would be over quickly. It was just a formality.

Only this time it wasn't.

"I've found a small lump above your right breast. Have *you* noticed it, Patti? Does it hurt when I press here?"

No, she had not and no, it did not.

"Probably nothing," the doctor spoke in a smooth voice. "But it needs to be checked. I want you to see a surgeon. In the morning."

It couldn't wait a week, until after the holidays?

No it could not. "The sooner we find out it's nothing, the better." And closing her chart, in a voice still smooth, the casual words: "Hoping for a girl this time?"

First a biopsy. The news was not good.

Then a lumpectomy. The news was bad.

Finally, a mastectomy.

Patti had cancer. An evil, fast growing, aggressive cancer, one that was thriving—growing like crazy in fact, boosted minute by minute by the super-strength estrogen a pregnant body produces. It was a good thing they'd found it when they did, the doctors agreed, for left untreated Patti would have likely been dead in two years, maybe less.

Time was critical. Chemotherapy was indicated. The sooner the better. Immediate arrangements would be made. And of course the pregnancy would have to be sacrificed.

"Excuse me? *Sacrificed?*"

Abortion. Standard in cases like this. Once the procedure was done, chemotherapy could be started and the abundant estrogens that were, *at this very moment*, fueling the aggressive cancer and encouraging its rapid growth, would naturally be reduced.

Perhaps someday, she could have another baby. After all, she *did* already have a child. Not all women were so lucky.

"Lucky?" Patti found her voice. What was lucky was this pregnancy. Luck nothing! If not for this baby, for this unexpected, unplanned *gift from God* she would not have known about the cancer. Casual about monthly self-examination, Patti was positive she would not have found the lump. This pregnancy, this baby, had saved *her* life, and she would not stop *its* life. Would not.

"You are making a very unwise decision," her doctor was not pleased. "Treatment will have to be delayed if you continue this pregnancy, and waiting will give the cancer time to spread. The course will be difficult even if you do end the pregnancy. It will be terribly complicated if you choose to continue it."

But Patti *did* choose. And so she found a different doctor, one who shared her faith and who told her she would do everything possible to save both her *and* the baby. "But make no mistake," she stressed to Patti and Danny, "continuing the pregnancy poses a risk to Patti, and to the baby as well."

Patti believed she could do it.

With God's help.

She also told them, "Ask everyone you know to pray. Hard."

And so we did.

No matter how or when it was administered, the chemotherapy necessary to save Patti's life posed a grave risk to her unborn baby. It could bring on premature labor, possibly miscarriage, might cause serious birth defects. But by stalling until she was into her second trimester, then abruptly stopping the drugs during the third trimester, the risks could be minimized. And so, the very day that Patti's pregnancy passed the one-third mark, her body was poked with needles and threaded with tubes and bombarded with cancer-fighting drugs—massive doses of them.

The course of chemotherapy was harder than she thought it would be and, miserably ill, Patti had to spend days in a hospital bed. The anti-cancer drugs made her pale and sick and too weak to care for Anthony. She found it difficult to eat enough to nourish the baby, and almost overnight, her hair fell out.

Patti remembered how she'd felt fat and unattractive during her pregnancy with Anthony. She'd not thought her maternity clothes flattering and she'd worried over stretch marks; rubbed them with cream. This time, standing alone and naked in front of the bathroom mirror, bald, one-breasted, and bulging-bellied, she wondered if she even looked human.

Once Patti reached the end of her second trimester, chemotherapy was, as planned, stopped. She was so glad it was over, she felt as if she'd finally reached an impossible goal. Despite her own fight against the cancer, Patti could only think of what the drugs might have done to her child, the unborn baby who she believed had saved her life.

But every kick of the baby she felt, every pound she gained, every normal sonogram—sonograms that showed the baby to be a little boy—*did* give her hope. And the bigger Patti's belly grew, the more she pressed her doctor, "Tell me, what are the chances that the baby's alright, that everything is okay?"

The doctor was kind, understood Patti's fears, in fact *shared* every one of them, but could give her no concrete answers, no real assurances, only brutal honesty. "We won't know anything until the baby is born and there is no point in guessing. We simply have to wait and see. Keep praying for the best, Patti."

Only days before Patti's due date, the doctor finally told her, "You know that the chemotherapy caused you to lose your hair. If it has adversely affected your baby, he too, will have lost his hair. If that has happened, it will not be a surprise. Whatever problems the baby might have, we will be ready to deal with them."

"*But,* if your baby is born with hair, it will be a very good sign that he has not been hurt by the drugs you took."

"Hair," Patti repeated. And from that moment on, she could think of nothing else.

Two days later, a carefully courageous Patti was wheeled into delivery. While she was breathing and pushing and sweating and straining, friends and family, waiting across the hall, spent the hours pacing and praying and drinking endless cups of vending machine coffee.

And finally, with one last push, the baby emerged.

"It's a boy alright," the doctor announced.

"Ten fingers and toes," a nurse informed.

"A chubby little guy," commented the anesthesiologist.

"But does he have . . . ? Does he have—?" An exhausted Patti panted and cried. "Does he have any hair?"

"See for yourself." And her baby, the child who'd maybe saved her life, the child who she'd risked her own life to save, was finally, *finally,* placed gently in her arms. Patti lifted the blanket and touched his sweet face, pulled back the blanket and held her breath.

But there was no need.

For the head of her baby, a child she and Danny would give the name Joseph, was covered—*covered*—with not just a few tiny strands, not just a wispy little fringe, but a full glorious crown of thick, black hair.

"Most hair I've ever seen on a newborn baby," said her doctor, a catch in her voice. "A full head of hair. Thanks be to God."

Indeed.

❧ ❧

This morning I phoned my friend Danna. She's Patti's mom and Joseph's grandma. Even though I've prayed for Patti, I've yet to meet her in person. "Danna," I began, "I don't know Patti, can't imagine how she must feel about all that's happened these past few months. I respect her privacy, but I would really like to tell her story. Do you think she would mind?"

Danna did not hesitate. "I think Patti would be honored. And if telling her story would encourage someone else, then I *know* she would approve."

"Patti," I'd like to tell her, "you've already encouraged us." Believe me. You already have.

I prayed for this child
and the LORD has granted me what I asked of him.
1 SAMUEL 1:27

CHAPTER THREE

Bear One Another's Burdens

*M*y friend Jeanna once observed, "Annette, somehow you manage to get around to actually *doing* all those crazy things other people think about but never have the nerve to try." Then she shook her head and laughed. "And you like change more than any person I know."

Jeanna and I have been friends so long—since we were teenagers—that I can't remember if she was speaking those words in reference to the time I mailed her a picture of my new never-before-seen-in-nature hair color or the afternoon I phoned to tell her the news that our first foster child had arrived.

Whatever the occasion, she was right. For while many folks are uncomfortable with change—don't like it *at all*, truth be told—I find routine and predictability almost unbearable, a fact borne witness to by my résumé's three-page listing of past jobs. I'm easily enticed by something new and different, something I've never tried or tasted, somewhere I've never been, someplace I've never seen.

And while I've had wonderful experiences and though I hold dear many incredible memories, my life choices have not come without trade-offs. Our family has moved more than a dozen times and we have fewer community roots and close ties than I would wish for. Realizing how many years we lack paying off our mortgage, I wonder if we'll ever stay in one place long enough to own a house free and clear. And I've never held a supervisory position at work. For while I'm a good employee, and receive excellent six-month and sometimes even yearly evaluations, I've yet to stay in one position long enough to be promoted.

Now my friend Jeanna, she *loves* predictability. Does *not* like change. She and her childhood sweetheart, husband Jack, have resided in only three towns since their marriage almost two decades ago. They married in, and continue to attend, the church where Jeanna grew up. She has worn her wavy brown hair in a tidy French braid for as long as I can remember, and her favorite meal—chicken fried steak and a loaded baked potato—is the same one she preferred in college.

Much can be said in defense of Jeanna's stable lifestyle. Due in great part to a stick-to-it attitude, she and her husband live almost debt-free. Good planning means that their bank account always holds money they've set aside for rainy days and Christmas presents. Jeanna enjoys the complete trust of the owner of the jewelry store where she works—a trust unheard of between shop owners and their employees, but one she's earned over the fifteen years she's worked there. And I admit to feeling a bit wistful when, while visiting, I observe up close the sense of belonging she enjoys living in the same town where she and her brothers and sister grew up.

Jeanna and I both married when we were twenty years old. True to my nature, a husband wasn't nearly enough excitement. To liven things up a bit, I gave birth to our son shortly before our second anniversary. A baby daughter arrived four years later.

Jeanna, on the other hand, ever cautious about things untried, eased into motherhood at a slower pace. And though I frequently pestered her about what they were waiting for, she and Jack enjoyed several years alone before deciding to have children. It was not until they had celebrated their fifth anniversary they concluded the time was right to have a baby.

But once she and Jack did decide to start a family, *they were ready*.

It was not to be that simple.

Jeanna could become pregnant all right. Easily. She just couldn't stay that way. And so while I tended to my four-year-old son and my newborn daughter, while her younger sister conceived her third child, while the *whole world* seemed to walk around pregnant, Jeanna suffered miscarriages. One after another.

And for the first time ever, I did not know how to be there for my friend. I tried and tried, but I had no idea what to say to her. I'm sure my almost daily long distance phone calls (the ones with the noises of my laughing and crying children in the background) provided no comfort to her.

I said all those things one says when something tragic and unfair and unexplainable happens to a friend. And my words were meaningless to her.

Each time she lost a baby I sent flowers to the hospital and letters and cards to her house. I mailed her pretty night-gowns and inspirational books and batches of her favorite oatmeal raisin cookies.

Once I even sent her a pair of red, on-sale, high-heeled sandals.

But nothing, nothing I nor anyone else did eased her grief. And so it felt for me, that for those years—and Jeanna's unsuccessful quest for motherhood did in fact stretch into years—my dearest friend was gone. She had walled herself up in this place, this little room, into which no one could come.

Jeanna didn't call and didn't write. She forgot my birthday and skipped her annual week-long visit to my house.

I missed her.

I did not understand.

And selfishly, I wanted her back

Canton, Texas claims to host the world's largest flea market. Known by locals as First Monday Trades Day, the festive, monthly, four-day event sprawls across acres and acres of the small town and attracts thousands of visitors from all over the nation.

"Going to Canton?" my friends and I ask each other as the end of each month draws near. "This is Canton weekend. Remember?"

"Gonna try to go," we answer. "Hoping to." Canton is fun. There are antiques and art and crafts and junk and great food. You can go to Canton with a group of friends and spend a lot of money or you can go with only cash enough for lunch and still have a great time. Temperate Texas weather means shoppers and lookers alike can enjoy Canton almost twelve months of the year.

I called Jeanna and invited her to join me at the flea market, and she agreed to plan her visit around Canton weekend. We like to go on Friday when it's less crowded. Not wanting to miss a thing, we set out early that morning and arrived by eight o'clock. Neither of us had anything specific in mind to purchase, but over weeks of planning the outing, we'd each managed to sock away a little money to spend.

The two of us had been roaming the aisles, poking around in eye-catching booths for less than an hour, when Jeanna spotted an antique iron, the kind a pioneer woman might have heated in a wood stove before using it to her crease the sleeves of her husband's Sunday shirt.

Jeanna had to have it.

"It will look so cute next to my grandmother's old wooden ironing board," she explained. "And it's priced almost half of what I was expecting to pay for an iron—if I ever found one."

So Jeanna bought the iron. The booth owner wrapped it up in newspaper and Jeanna placed it in the bottom of her canvas tote bag. "Do you think we could make a quick trip to the car?" she asked. "This iron is really heavy."

Not wanting to take time out to make the twenty-minute walk to the parking lot, I discouraged her. "Oh, let's wait till after lunch. Then we can take anything else we've bought at the same time. Make one trip. Don't worry, when you get tired, just let me know and I'll carry your bag. We'll take turns. Okay?"

She agreed.

About an hour later, Jeanna's shoulder began to sag. She set the bag on the ground and rotated her arm uncomfortably. "Annette, that iron is *really* heavy. Could you carry it awhile?"

Of course. No problem, I thought.

Big problem.

The bag, with the iron in it, must have weighed ten pounds. *Ten pounds!* Not only was it heavy, but the way the iron rested in the bag, every time I took a step it swung wildly and knocked against the side of my calf. No matter how I tried to lug it, which position or which hand I tried, I was miserable.

"Jeanna," I complained. "Why didn't you tell me how heavy this was? I had no idea. If I'd known, we would have gone straight to the car."

But Jeanna just smiled and shrugged, *and* let me keep carrying her bag.

❧ ❧

Often, I think I understand what those I love are going through. I can see their burdens, can imagine what it must be like to bear them, can even make generous offers to help. Yet no matter how I may assume I know how someone else feels, until I have carried that same burden in my own arms, I've learned that *I don't understand.*

And so there are two lessons I learned from my friend Jeanna (who by the way did go on to have two beautiful, healthy children) on that sunny fall day in Canton, Texas:

When someone tells you their load is heavy, believe them. And when they want to go to the car, lead the way.

I removed the burden from their shoulders.

PSALM 81:6

CHAPTER FOUR

Don't Ask Questions

*S*idney could *always* be counted on. She and Helen, friends since third grade, met every summer weeknight after supper. Together they jogged a two-mile loop around the Junior High School, through the park, and back to Sidney's house. Occasionally they were chased by dogs and often they were offered rides. Sweating and gasping, Helen was often tempted to stumble right to a generous passerby's air-conditioned car, buckle up, and head on home. Not Sidney. She virtuously chanted encouragement and instruction to Helen as they jogged. "Head up. Feet flat. Back straight. Come on! You can do it!"

Their route was generally a safe one. Only once did they feel afraid—the time when five rowdy young men, packed in a red Mustang, followed slowly behind their jiggling bottoms for two blocks, whistling and shouting lewd comments. Luckily, a patrolling policeman happened by at just the right time. The sight of him cooled the men's beer-fueled lust and they sped away. Neither woman mentioned the incident to her husband, but from then on, Sidney jogged with a silver meat fork tucked into the waistband of her shorts.

Like always, Sidney knew how to handle any situation. Not Helen. Lacking, among other things, the most basic of domestic instincts, she tended to be casual about things like clean undershorts and fresh milk, well-made beds and a swept-off front porch. Helen tried, really tried, to manage her household well, but often found herself bringing in clothes off the line at midnight and trying at six o'clock in the evening to make husband Nathan's supper from a hard-as-rock, unthawed chicken.

And though Nathan was a patient man, a tolerant man, it was he who first suggested, then gently insisted, that his wife hire someone to help with the house.

Helen was reluctant. Didn't like the idea. Told her husband she didn't know how to go about finding domestic help.

"Ask Sidney," he urged. "She'll know someone. Ask her. Tonight."

Predictably, when queried about a maid for Helen and Nathan, Sidney responded with a quick recommendation. "Alice Bay. About forty. Black woman. Hard worker. Out of a job since Mrs. Avery went to the nursing home last month. She'll be perfect."

"Don't you know anyone else?" Helen twisted her hands in her lap.

Sidney didn't. And so phone calls were placed and arrangements were made and before she knew it, Helen had become Alice Bay's employer.

Alice, efficient, energetic, and grateful to have a job, took Helen and Nathan's chaotic household and, within a few days, had it smoothed right out. Helen no longer found herself bringing board-stiff, long-dried clothes in off the line after dark, and Nathan enjoyed sweet, not sour, milk on his corn flakes. Crisp sheets appeared on the beds and soft towels in the bathroom. The front porch was swept clean and the refrigerator stocked with fresh food.

"Now, isn't it nice having help?" Nathan asked.

"Don't you wish you'd done this a long time ago?" Sidney asked.

No, it wasn't. And no, she didn't.

For though she liked the effect Alice had on her household, Helen, young and white-skinned, had always considered herself to be a progressive thinker, to be a *liberal* even. And she hated, truly *hated,* being the employer of middle-aged, brown-skinned Alice.

It didn't feel right.

So she tried to appease her distaste with repeated awkward and unsuccessful attempts at friendship. Trying to strike up conversations, she asked Alice about her family, talked about the weather, commented on the rising price of tomatoes. But her efforts were useless. Though Alice politely, but stiffly, answered Helen's questions, she offered no other response to her employer's friendly overtures.

Even though Helen asked Alice to call her and Nathan by their first names, she continued to address them as "Mr. and Mrs. Hudson," and she always answered them with "yes ma'am," and "no sir." She tolerated, but did not return, Helen's cheery morning greetings—greetings that might possibly have been appropriate for important company but which were a bit overdone considering that, within the hour, Alice would be scouring Helen's toilet and rinsing out her lingerie in cold water and Woolite.

The harder Helen tried, the more Alice withdrew from her.

"I don't know why she doesn't like me," Helen whined to Sidney during their evening jog. "I haven't done anything to offend her. I've tried to be nice."

Only when Alice became pregnant with her fifth child did she soften a bit toward Helen. She agreed, each afternoon, to rest a few minutes with her feet up, was grateful for the milk Helen supplied for her to drink with her brought-from-home lunch, and laughed out loud when childless Helen told her not to hang out clothes on the line any more. Helen had heard that if a pregnant woman raised her arms over her head, the baby would be born with the cord around its neck.

"Not true," Alice assured her, shaking her head. "Not true at all."

Alice worked right up until the Saturday night her baby was born. When she did not show up for work on the following Monday, Helen learned of the baby's birth. And she could not, would not, keep herself from going over to Alice's house.

"Not a good idea, honey," Nathan tried to tell her.

"What are you thinking, Helen?" Sidney exclaimed.

Helen would not, did not, listen. She packed up a gift-wrapped baby blanket and a freshly baked apple cake, a pot roast, and a pot of peas and drove herself across town to Alice's house.

She was met at the door by Alice's oldest boy. Tall and stony-faced, he looked her up and down before letting her in. Helen stood inside the doorway, clutched her offerings, and admitted with *great* unease that Nathan and Sidney had been right.

This intrusion had not been a good idea. At all.

Unsure what to do, she put the food in the refrigerator and placed the gift-wrapped blanket on the table before being led by yet another child back to the bedroom. It took a minute for her eyes to adjust to the dim room and to see Alice and the baby, propped up in bed.

"I wanted to see you, to see the baby. I . . . I brought you some supper. Thought you might not feel like cooking."

"Thank you," Alice spoke stiffly. "Nice of you. Be back to work as soon as I can."

"Oh, don't worry about that. You can come back whenever you're ready. There's no hurry. Really."

No answer. Just awkward silence.

Helen saw herself out.

Alice and I are friends. Sort of. She's not a maid any more. In fact, though she's past retirement age, she owns and runs a downtown shop. I often stop by to browse and chat. Because I ask, because she knows that *I want to know,* occasionally Alice tells me of the struggles she's faced as a black woman. Sometimes the stories she tells me are painful to hear. I want to argue with her, to insist, "That can't be true! That didn't *really* happen!" Sometimes I want to change the subject. I feel the urge to cover my ears.

But I don't. I sit quietly and I listen.

When Alice was twenty years old, she moved to a new town. Moved from Dallas, a large modern city, to a much smaller town in a rural area one hundred miles away. She had family there.

Once she'd settled in, Alice called the local hospital to inquire of the director of nursing about a position as a nurse's aide. She'd loved working as an aide in a big Dallas hospital, had been told over and over by appreciative staff and patients that she had a gift for it. Alice secretly dreamed of someday going to nursing school.

"Yes," she was told by the friendly-voiced nursing director. "We're hiring. Very short-staffed right now. Looking for several good people."

"Seven years experience? Three letters of recommendation, two of them from doctors? Excellent!"

"Could you interview this afternoon? Just a formality of course. We'll get you started right away."

"Four o'clock?"

"Wonderful!"

And so young Alice dressed with care, fixed her hair just so, shined her shoes, and arrived at the hospital ten minutes early. *The hospital was hiring!* She couldn't believe her luck.

Alice, waiting for her appointment just outside the director's office in a slick vinyl chair, absently flipped through old magazines and wondered to what area in this hospital she would be assigned. *Perhaps labor and delivery ... maybe the emergency room ... then again in such a small place she'd probably be expected to work all over ...*

It would be none of those.

Once seated in the office, she knew something was wrong.

The director looked over Alice's application, read her letters of recommendation, shifted uncomfortably in her chair, and repeatedly cleared her throat. Alice watched as the woman's hands bent and twisted a paper clip. Saw when the wire clip broke in two.

"Alice," the woman spoke finally, "your application looks wonderful. I've never read such glowing letters of recommendation. Obviously, you're a very good worker. No doubt you are someone who takes good care of your patients. But we do have a problem."

Alice sat stone still, legs crossed at the ankle. Felt her hands grow moist.

"This is a small town. Things are not the same here as they are in Dallas. People in this town hold to the old ways. And it is the policy of this hospital—a policy set by the hospital board—not to hire Negroes for nursing duties. When you called, I could not tell by your voice that you were . . ." her voice trailed off. "Negroes who live here are aware of the policy. Being new to town, you had no way of knowing. I am sorry. I can offer you a job in the kitchen or you could work in the laundry."

❧ ❦❧

At this moment I can hear muffled giggles and loud music coming from my daughter's closed bedroom door. She has friends over to spend the night. There will be half a dozen teenage bodies sprawled in sleeping bags on my living room floor tonight. Among those sleeping figures will be Helen's daughter and Alice's granddaughter. They are two of my daughter's best friends. The three of them are, in fact, practically inseparable.

I know how teenage girls are. I don't ask a lot of questions. But from what I see, from what I quietly observe, the fact that they are not all of the same race seems to be of little concern to them, at least when it comes to their friendships.

I am glad.

And though I don't ask a lot of questions, so, I think, are Helen and Alice.

I have called you friends.
JOHN 15:15

CHAPTER FIVE

Change Reaction

*M*y friend Karey gives good advice. I drove to church out-of-sorts, grumpy, and grumbly one sunny Sunday last fall. My panty hose had twisted and my skirt felt too tight. My head hurt *and* I'd just agreed to fill in for a sick nursery worker during morning worship. Even worse, I wasn't just having a bad day—I was having a bad month. Chatting with my friend in the hallway outside the Young Marrieds Sunday School classroom, I confided, "Karey, I feel just rotten and I don't know what to do. I don't like my husband or my children or my job or my house. I'm sick of this town and I'm not even crazy about this church. What's wrong with me?"

"Why Annette, there is not one thing wrong with you," Karey's sweet west-Texas drawl soothed me. "I get that way myself. Those feelings are normal as can be. You just need a change."

A change? I mused. *New husband? . . . No. . . . New children? . . . No. . . . New house? . . . Probably not. . . . New job? . . . Maybe. . . . My mind was moving ahead now. . . . Perhaps I should think about going back to school. . . . or maybe getting away for a few days . . . A short trip would be nice. . . .*

"What you need," Karey interrupted and advised with *total* conviction, "what will get you right out of this mood—is a new haircut."

When my husband's boss asked him *why in the world* our busy family was planning to host a foreign exchange student, Randy shrugged and answered, "My wife just doesn't have enough to do." His answer wasn't exactly accurate. Truth is, I have *plenty* to do, I just want to do something else.

I like change.

The next week, Nils, a slim, six-foot, blond German teenager became our new son-for-a-year. On his first evening in our home, to celebrate his arrival, I prepared a festive meal, including a decorated cake inscribed *Welcome to Texas*. I expected our new son to be impressed. But the sweltering August heat, difficult communication, and a serious case of homesickness seemed to overwhelm. Sixteen-year-old Nils kept his eyes down and his voice low and ate very little. I pretended not to notice how his hands trembled as he cut the first piece of cake.

Overnight, Nils had to acclimate to near 100% humidity, learn to decipher our puzzling Texas slang, and deal with the sudden separation from his parents.

Our family had its own adjustments to make. Russell, for the year, would share his room and one small closet with Nils. Rachel would now compete with not one, but two big brothers for a few coveted minutes in the bathroom each morning. My trips to the grocery store would become more frequent when I discovered that jumbo-size boxes of Cheerios and gallon jugs of orange juice disappeared overnight. Randy, who helped with laundry, would find many extra loads of sweaty T-shirts and smelly gym socks to wash.

Thankfully Nils, once the initial adjustment was made, proved to be quiet, polite, and eager to do what was expected of him. He studied several hours each night and brought home excellent grades. Though Randy and I encouraged him to participate in extracurricular school activities (Russell and Rachel were involved in a myriad of after-class projects), he chose instead to spend his free time close to home, shooting hundreds of baskets through our backyard hoop, watching televised American sports, and learning to cook his favorite American foods: chicken quesadillas and Rice Krispy treats.

Because on weekdays he and I arrived home earlier than the rest of the family, Nils and I routinely watched the evening news together. Keenly interested in both world and national affairs, he always had questions for me—some of which, I admit, I struggled to answer.

It was after viewing a lengthy feature report about the U.S. Army that Nils asked me how the American military was staffed. I explained that at the present time in history, people served voluntarily, but that the government had the right to institute a system called "the draft." In that case, men would be required to go and serve.

Nils' jaw tightened and his face turned pale. "If *my* government tried to make *me* fight, I would run away and hide from them."

I held my tongue but inwardly winced at his statement. Finally, choosing my words carefully, I spoke. "In America, most citizens believe we should all be willing to fight for our freedom, to sacrifice for the liberty of each other. If there was a war, I would be terribly frightened and upset, but I would expect Russell to be ready to serve our country. Americans believe in what we call *patriotism*."

"In my country, if you call yourself a patriot, then you are also a Nazi," was Nils' adamant reply.

Every month that year, the local foreign exchange program director, a retired businessman named George, held a party for the students and their host families. We attended several of these get-togethers and I enjoyed them immensely. I found it interesting to meet like-minded families and to hear how things were going in their households.

George was careful not to interfere in our normal family life, but he wanted to ensure a positive experience for everyone involved and to deal quickly with any problems between host families and exchange students. So every few weeks he phoned us at home. George would talk first to Randy or me, ask if everything was going well, and then speak privately to Nils.

"I don't like George." Nils stated abruptly after one of these conversations. "He is a racist."

"George? A *racist?*"

No way. George volunteered hours and hours of his time, was devoted to a program whose primary goal was to increase understanding between nations, one family at a time.

"Nils, I agree that George is a little odd. He talks a lot, and he dresses kind of funny, but what makes you say he's a racist?"

"He thinks German students are better than other kids."

"*What?*"

"At our first meeting, when all the students first came to Texas, George told all of us that he only sponsors German students. He thinks other students, like French or Japanese or Spanish kids, aren't as smart or as talented or don't behave as well as Germans. George says that only German students are good. Every time he calls me, he says it again and again and again. He is a racist and I don't like him."

I was angry.

A well-known white supremacy group planned to hold a rally in our peaceful little town. No long-time community leaders could remember such a gathering being held before, and no one could guess what had precipitated the sudden scheduling of such a hateful event.

Why now? I fumed. *Why this, of all years. I want Nils to see the very best of the United States, to see the love and compassion of Americans. I don't want him to see this ignorance and ugliness, this cowardly exploitation of free speech.*

I was *angry,* but Nils—well Nils was absolutely *livid* when he heard about the rally.

"What are we going to do about this?" he demanded of me. "We have to do something." His white-knuckled hand stabbed at the town newspaper's descriptive headline and his voice quivered with fury.

As I struggled to explain, groped for some kind of an answer, my eyes fell upon a treasured tabletop photo grouping of the foster children Randy and I have cared for. Their faces, ranging in hue from palest white to darkest brown, stared at me. I remembered them and their sweetness and recalled the hateful reactions some people displayed toward us while we were a multi-racial family.

I drew a long breath.

"The only thing we *can* do is ignore the whole thing. We will stay away from downtown the whole day of the rally. What this group wants most is our attention. If no one goes to their gathering, if no one hears their speeches, then it will be a failure for them. The best thing we can do is do nothing."

Nils did *not* agree. In a teeth-clenched response, he paraphrased words spoken by his favorite American president, a young leader who was slain many years ago. "When good people ignore bad things, the bad things will get worse."

🍃

What can we do about prejudice, hatred, and bigotry? After all these years, it continues to be an embarrassing, pervasive problem in our nation.

Randy and I have attempted to teach our children, both by our words and our actions, to love and understand all people. We've tried to expose them to families different from ours, to cultivate friends who have different skin colors, cultures, and economic and educational levels than we have. Inviting Nils into our home was one such attempt to broaden our family's understanding.

And Nils did just that. We learned from his readiness to rebel should he be asked to fight a battle he believed was wrong, his strong recoil from the notion that some groups are superior to others, and his youthful, courageous notion that *good people should do something.*

Nils returned to his home in Germany more than two years ago. He went back to his life with his parents and we became, once again, a family of four, whose members (at least for a while) all share the same last name. We slipped easily back into our routines and so did he. As it should, life goes on for him and for us. But in spite of our predictable, rapid returns to normalcy, it is because of a year together that we are all different. A small part of him, and of us, will never be the same.

And so I remain convinced, change is good.

We will be changed.
1 CORINTHIANS 15:52

CHAPTER SIX

Robin's Baby

Sunday morning church services have historically presented logistical challenges for mothers of small children. I remember one particular morning when our son was a newborn. At the time, we owned one car, and on that particular Sunday morning Randy needed a ride to the hospital where he worked. So I rose early, nursed the baby, dressed him and me, and took Randy to work. Once home, I bathed Russell and me, dressed us both again, nursed him again, changed him, ate my breakfast and curled my hair, nursed him and changed him again. And nursed him again.

Finally, *hours and hours* after I'd gotten up, we made it to worship. I slipped into a back pew, set the diaper bag down, hoisted Russell up on my shoulder, took a deep breath, and looked down to see that my dress was on backwards.

Russell was unusually wriggly and cranky that morning and I struggled to keep him from disturbing the worshippers around us. After a wet-diapered, spit up-smelling, not-very-successful hour, I was exhausted. And though, mercifully, the service was over early and we had made it without causing a major disturbance, I was left feeling irritable and frustrated, even close to tears.

Why had I even bothered to come? I wondered and fumed. *There is no point in me even being here.*

At that very minute a sweet-faced, soft-haired older woman appeared at my elbow. I'll never forget the woman's unusual name—Bea Honey. And a *honey* she was. I look back now and I think that perhaps she was an angel, albeit cleverly disguised, in sling-back shoes and a polyester shift.

It was as if she had read my mind.

"You know dear," she soothed, "it's so hard to worship with a little one on your lap and I imagine that sometimes you get very little out of coming to church." She stroked Russell's cheek and patted my arm. "But at least," her eyes twinkled conspiratorially, "today you let the devil know which side you're on!"

Thankfully, I had Wednesday Women's Bible class to look forward to. Child care was provided and I usually arrived on time. I loved the class. It was attended by about thirty young mothers like me and was taught by a lovely grandmother, the wife of a well-respected church leader.

"Today," the teacher began one morning, "we're going to begin a study of Old Testament women: how they lived, what their concerns were, and how God played a part in their lives." She continued, "One of the first things you'll notice about women back then was that they most often had very large families. They gave birth to lots of children." She looked around the room with warmth and understanding but spoke a bit shyly. "Women of long ago didn't have the ability to *plan* their families, to choose the sizes of their families like mothers of today."

She paused to look at her notes, and at that very moment, six puffy-ankled, elastic-stretched-out, unexpectedly pregnant women looked at her, then at each other, and burst out laughing.

"Well," the dear woman blushed, "perhaps things haven't changed that much after all."

My friend Robin is the happy mother of two rowdy, almost-grown-up boys. When they were little she played with them, read to them, scolded, and adored them. She bought them cowboy outfits and water guns, farm sets and race cars, and read stories to them about policemen and firemen and turtles and snakes. She decorated their rooms in primary colors and put up shelves for their Legos, and she learned to live with a toilet seat that was never left down.

Fiercely, wildly, she loved her boys, but deep, deep down inside she *longed* for a little girl.

When Robin held my frilly-shoed, hair-ribboned, sweet-smelling baby girl, when she gazed into the eyelet-draped room I'd prepared for a pink and white princess, she'd sigh and sigh and say again and again, "I just hope my next one's a girl."

Well, when The Test came back positive (every woman of childbearing age knows of which test I speak), Robin was ecstatic. And when a second trimester sonogram showed that Robin's baby was, in fact a girl—well she was just tickled pastel, you could say.

After the sonogram, with just four months to prepare, both Robin and her checkbook got busy. She bought bonnets and booties and ribbons and roses. She painted and papered and stitched and stenciled and created a feminine, fairy-tale nursery that left the males in her family shaking their heads in wonder.

And she dreamed. Of tea parties and petticoats and portraits in lace. Of French braids and bangs and ruffled white tights.

Robin called me almost every morning to ask my opinion on the latest names she was considering for the baby. She had asked her husband what he thought they should name her and been aghast when the poor man innocently suggested Tracy Lynn or Kerry Rae. *This* baby, she was sure, this little girl of hers, would be the prettiest thing in the world and as such, *must* have a name of equal beauty and femininity. She poured over name books for weeks but had trouble deciding between Elizabeth or Emily, Catherine or Camille.

Robin's husband—a fine man, a strong man, a committed family man—had but one glaring flaw. The man was squeamish. Had a history of fainting, in fact, at the sight of blood. So it was decided that I, the Friend Who Is A Nurse, would stand in as labor coach.

Robin and I attended Lamaze classes, practiced her breathing, and went over her checklist of things to pack for the hospital. Finally the day arrived and after a long and difficult delivery—one in which Robin abandoned her role as natural childbirth evangelist to take all the pain-killing drugs she was able to extort from her kindhearted but conservative obstetrician—her long awaited baby emerged into the light.

She had her girl.

The one she'd dreamed of.

Forever.

Sort of . . .

The doctor cut the cord and a nurse placed the baby on Robin's chest. I looked at the newborn and smiled at the sight of the long and skinny, red-faced, wet little thing. Her bald head, after the long delivery, was temporarily and not surprisingly—but unfortunately—shaped like a lopsided pear. She looked a bit like a wrinkled old man.

Robin, still groggy from the medication, wrapped her arms around her daughter, stroked her little wrinkled-up brow, kissed her tiny hand, and began to weep.

I stood beside her and watched. *Why, she's just overcome with joy,* I thought. A tear slid down my cheek. *A daughter is such a wonderful thing!*

"Oh, oh, oh," Robin cried, interrupting my melodramatic musings. "I prayed and I prayed for God to give me a little girl." She sniffed and she sobbed and wiped her nose with the back of her hand. "And He sent me," sniff, sniff, "the ugliest one He had! Wahhhh!"

🙌 🙌

I'm almost forty years old now and making it through church on Sunday isn't much of a challenge anymore. Eighteen-year-old Russell will start college in the fall and my baby girl is in Junior High. Randy and I no longer belong in the Young Marrieds Sunday School class and we don't have to hire a sitter when we go to the movies on Friday night.

Robin's baby girl, the object of her drug-induced disappointment so many years ago, turned out to be a beautiful young woman. Her head is no longer shaped anything like a pear and her skin is no longer wrinkled and red. She plays the piano and writes poetry and models on Saturdays at a downtown department store.

Today when I see young mothers and mothers-to-be, their lives wrapped up in diapers and teething and car seats and croup, I realize with a bit of shock that part of my life is over. Gone for good.

But I confess, *I'm really sort of glad.* Raising babies and toddlers was exciting and rewarding and fulfilling and fun, but it was *hard!*

These days when I see a young mother struggling and tired after wrestling through church, I remember Mrs. Honey and her words of encouragement. And so I take that baby and I tickle that toddler and I pat that mother's arm, and I tell her she's doing a great job. And whether she smiles or she cries or she grits her teeth, I hug her and I tell her it will all soon be over.

Yes.

Way too soon.

It will all be over.

Her children arise and call her blessed.
PROVERBS 31:28

PART TWO

All in the Family

CHAPTER SEVEN

Setting the Table

arly in my parents' forty-year marriage, my dad hauled home, in the back of his muddy pickup truck, an old, beat-up-looking oak table. Dad sold livestock feed. While driving his assigned route of farm stores one afternoon, taking the back roads wherever possible, he drove up on an auction in progress. Observing the cluster of pickups and cattle trailers and always on the lookout for folks who might be encouraged to use his product, he stopped and joined the crowd around the auctioneer. Dad did not intend to buy anything, but the table caught his eye. When it went up on the block, he surprised himself by bidding on it. Though purchased at a fair price, the table cost was enough to stretch a newlywed budget, and as he loaded it, he sheepishly wondered if my mom would even like it.

The table had been stored in a barn for several seasons and was covered with a thick coat of grime and several layers of sticky varnish. But my mom took it to a furniture restorer and within a few weeks the table was returned, transformed into a stunning, unusual piece of furniture. Crafted of honey-colored oak, supported by five ornately carved legs, the table is so heavily crafted it requires both my mom and my dad to pull it open to its full length.

Kept polished to a mellow, gleaming finish, the table was, and continues to be, a prominent fixture in the household that reared my two brothers and me. If tables could talk, this one could tell about much it has witnessed since its humble entrance into the family. It would tell about a home, about years of growth and changes, about good times and tough ones. Most of all, the table would tell about the love manifested in the endless hospitality extended by my mom and dad.

Although some fabulous meals have been served on it, the people and the diversity of activities undertaken as our family evolved are what make this table's story so rich and unique. A variety of fine shoes and bare feet, both of assorted sizes and colors, have rested under its oak leaves.

The table has watched a series of boyfriends and girl-friends nervously pass casseroles under my dad's intentionally intimidating gaze. Gradually, and to his great relief, the table saw two daughters-in-law and a son-in-law replace the dizzying choice of romantic companions entertained by the kids in the family.

As the years passed, we female members of the clan intermittently found scooting close to the table difficult because of baby-blossomed bellies. As the family has matured, the variety of chairs gathered around the table have included both highchairs and wheelchairs. Recently, the table witnessed the number of needed seats diminish as the oldest members of four generations now sit at a heavenly table instead of an earthly one.

Despite its elegant appearance, all manners of activities have taken place on the table's plastic-covered surface. When I was ten, my friends and I spent a memorably sticky December afternoon constructing miniature houses of graham crackers and royal icing. Only a few structures were actually completed, but the girls giggled and talked and enjoyed an afternoon some of my now grown-up women friends still remember.

Extended to its full length, the table provided the perfect flat surface for my mom to cut yards of fabric to be sewn into everything from chair pads and kitchen curtains to Easter dresses and even the wool suit my brother was married in. Other ventures crafted on its surface include paper and paste volcanoes, preschool finger paintings, and seventh grade bug collections.

Draped with lace and set with china and silver, the table was the setting for numerous fancy parties. Silent lessons about the equality of all people were taught to me when I saw my mother use the same finery for the baby shower she hosted for a hastily wed, new-to-the-community teenager that she used for the wedding shower thrown for a college-educated, prominent physician's daughter.

Frequently, large groups used the table as a buffet. When my brothers were young teens, the table was piled high with hamburgers and soft drinks for the junior high football team—all seventy hopeful members.

While a university student, one of my brothers developed a special friendship with a large group of students from Thailand. Two years in a row, he brought more than thirty students to the table for a long country weekend. To show their gratitude, the students prepared dinner for the family one evening. Though tasty, the feast they prepared was so spicy that even those of us raised on fiery Tex-Mex cuisine raced to the sink for water.

Summers brought the barely adult staff of a nearby youth camp to the table for my mother's famous chicken-fried steak and gravy. Late into the night, far-from-home staff members played cards and sorted laundry and wrote letters home—on the same table where earlier they'd eaten dinner.

Guests of diverse economic levels, educational backgrounds, races and nationalities have sat around the table.

A variety of topics have been discussed over coffee and cookies. The table has eavesdropped as my dad, a man holding thoughtful and sometimes conservative views, patiently listened to a brash college student explain the latest liberal political philosophy.

Friends have chuckled as jokes and stories were told. Business deals have been hammered out, college plans discussed, tears shed, and debates argued. Budgets have been made and blown, checkbooks balanced, and coupons clipped on top of it. Letters written, recipes copied, and order forms completed. All these activities, some mundane and some profound, have taken place on the old table my dad purchased so many years ago.

It's been several years since my brothers and I left our parents' house to begin our own homes, to begin building new memories and traditions. We are scattered miles apart and all of us find ourselves pursuing our own divergent lifestyles. But some things never change, and if you were to visit in each of our homes, you would find one thing that is the same.

We each have our own oak tables.

Bring in the table and set out what belongs on it.
Exodus 40:4

CHAPTER EIGHT

Second Helpings

andy's grandparents were rich. *Really* rich. He knew this to be true because of the bounty he observed every summer. Randy and his brother, Dale, and his sister, Diana, spent a week every summer at Grandmother and Granddad's house. Each year, he was more convinced of their wealth than ever. Consider the evidence: Grandmother's clear crystal candy dish was *not just for looks.* There was *actually* candy in it. Peppermints. The fruit bowl on the sideboard held not only apples, oranges, and bananas, but *seedless green grapes.* In the frosty freezer section of the refrigerator, there were stashed not just one, but *two* flavors of ice cream—*at the same time!* If that weren't enough to thoroughly convince any doubter of his grandparents' affluence, there, on the top shelf of the pantry, sat two boxes of real ice cream cones.

Granddad and Grandmother ate ice cream cones *any time they wanted to.*

The house Grandmother and Granddad lived in was such a big one that two families lived in it. Grandmother and Granddad lived in one half of the house, and Mrs. Chambers lived in the other half. She came over each morning to drink coffee with Grandmother and since she had a television, Grandmother went over to Mrs. Chamber's each afternoon to watch *As the World Turns*. Mrs. Chambers was nice, but she took long naps after lunch and it was difficult, while visiting for the week, to be quiet and not disturb her. Except for having to be quiet during Mrs. Chambers' naps, the weeks spent at Grandmother and Granddad's were, in Randy's opinion, perfect.

During their visits, Randy always slept in the back bedroom with Granddad, and Diana in the front bedroom with Grandmother. Dale had dibs on a cot in the living room. Every morning, Granddad had to get up early to go to work. He was in charge of a factory machine that forged precision holes in big metal pipes. To be on time for his early shift, he was up and on his way before the children got up. Randy vowed every night to be awake to tell Granddad goodbye, but it just never happened. Granddad had so perfected his tip-toed shave and dress-in-the-dark routine he disturbed no one. The only proof he left of being up and moving at all was his missing black lunchbox, absent from its prepacked-by-Grandmother position on top of the refrigerator.

Once the children got up, they ate breakfasts of oatmeal with lots of butter and white sugar. After washing and dressing in play clothes, Randy, Dale, and Diana romped the house with toys and games Grandmother liked to play. She was good at Dominos but really liked to play Bingo—especially when she got to be the caller. Grandmother also had some books for them to look at and a box of cardboard nursery rhyme pop-up scenes. Randy liked "Old King Cole" pretty well, but he wasn't too fond of "Hey Diddle Diddle." Something about that old cow jumping over the moon just didn't seem right.

After lunch, usually sandwiches and pound cake slices, the three children tried to play quietly. Randy and Dale helped Grandmother count, stack, and roll the pennies she collected all year in big half-gallon pickle jugs. Once the pennies were rolled, the heavy cylinders were fun to arrange and rearrange in shapes and designs on the floor. When their rambunctious penny play threatened to wear out the paper sleeves, Grandmother brought out the marble jar. Though none of the three ever mastered the *real* game of marbles, they orchestrated repeated complicated marble races. Luckily, the living room floor slanted perfectly to make for some close competitions. Randy's favorite marble, a purple one he nicknamed "Speedy," always won two out of every three races it ran in.

Bingo and marble races and playing with pennies were great, but the best part of the day, the *highlight* of the day by far, was waiting for Granddad to come home from work. Every afternoon at three o'clock sharp, Randy, Dale, and Diana went outside and sat on the wooden porch steps, side by side, chins-in-hands, to watch for him. Since Granddad didn't have a car, one of his friends drove him home each day, letting him off at the corner. The three children held contests to see who could spot Granddad first. Finally, after waiting for what seemed like forever, one of them, usually Randy, would glance up and see him striding down the street.

After enthusiastic rounds of homecoming hugs and kisses, Granddad slowly and with great ceremony handed his big black lunchbox over to the children. They pounced on it greedily, eager to see what would be inside. Since Granddad was never hungry enough to finish his lunchtime meal, there were always wonderful snacks left in his box. Each of the children claimed their favorites: Diana loved to eat the last corner of Granddad's sandwich and any cake crumbles that might be left. Randy munched left-behind peanut butter-smeared graham cracker sandwich halves. Only Dale lacked interest in the food gleanings. He went straight for Granddad's tall green thermos bottle, turned it up, and gulped the last half-cup of tepid, sugar-sweetened tea.

Grandmother was a good cook, but *nothing* she made for dinner *ever* tasted as good Granddad's lunchbox leavings.

After Granddad had bathed and changed into slacks and a pressed white shirt, the five of them sat down for an early supper. Once the meal was finished, Granddad got up, stretched, and asked if by chance, *anyone* was in the mood to play a game of tiddly winks. Always, three *someones* were definitely in the mood, so Granddad hunkered down over the coffee table and easily beat them one by one. He was a great tiddly wink player. The only time Randy saw Granddad get beat at tiddly winks was when he played Grandmother. She didn't play very often.

Evenings at Grandmother and Granddad's varied and were always fun. At least twice during the week the five of them walked to the park and enjoyed serious rounds of miniature golf. If it happened that local little league baseball teams were playing a tournament, they might stay and cheer a game or two. Since all the neighborhood churches held summer revivals, two or three evenings each week were spent hearing out-of-state evangelists preach powerful, pulpit-pounding sermons.

Once evening turned to night, Granddad would begin to yawn and announce it was time to head home. Early bedtimes marked reluctant ends to magical summer days.

❧ ❦

I love to hear my husband Randy reminisce about those weeks spent with his grandparents. He is a sentimental man, a man with a memory for great detail. I find the accounts he tells of his childhood days fascinating—the sleeping arrangements, the marble races, the penny rolls. I do admit that I find his memory of eating Granddad's leftover lunch scraps more than a bit curious.

"What," I ask him, "was the appeal of soggy sandwich corners, stale cake crumbles, and lukewarm tea?"

He is surprised and even a bit miffed when I voice my distaste. He thinks a moment before answering. "You don't understand," he finally tells me. "Those weren't leftovers. Not at all. Granddad always saved the best for us."

I hear his words and I comprehend my mistake.

And unexpectedly, I notice that I long for the taste of a graham cracker crumb. I thirst for a sip of tea.

The cheerful heart has a continual feast.

PROVERBS 15:15

CHAPTER NINE

Aunt Emma's Journey

During my Aunt Emma's senior year in high school, on the last Friday of each month, she grabbed her book bag, waved goodbye to her mother, and jumped on the school bus. Half an hour later the bus pulled up at the tiny rural school that she and her best friend Lucy attended. They hopped off the bus, huddled together, and glanced up and down to make sure no school official was looking. When they were reasonably sure the coast was clear, Lucy and Emma clutched their bags to their chests and ran the three long blocks to the town's Greyhound bus stop. There, out of breath, nervous and giggling, the two girls handed over their lunch money, hoarded up over weeks of hungry noon-times, and purchased round-trip tickets to Dallas, thirty miles away.

Once on the bus, with sweating, trembling hands and quick, ragged breaths, they smoothed their hair and powdered their noses and lined their lips with a shared and for-bidden-by-their-daddies ruby-red lipstick. When the bus made its stop in Dallas the two of them stepped slowly off and hoped they looked years older than they really were. Penniless after spending all of their money on bus tickets,

Emma and Lucy spent the next few hours leisurely roaming the sky-scraper-lined downtown streets, window shopping and dreaming of what it would be like to live in the city. By noon they both began to nervously check their watches, and no later than two o'clock, Lucy and Emma headed to the station and boarded their return bus.

Without fail, the two of them arrived back home, tired, sore-footed, and—again having had no lunch—starving, just in time to sneak onto the school bus and ride home as if it had been just another day in twelfth grade. Not once, and they made at least a dozen forbidden trips, did they get caught.

When Aunt Emma, now in her sixties, tells me of her teenage escapades, I find that I am both admiring of her bravado and appalled at her disobedience. Her behavior was risky and dangerous and, admittedly, I would be furious if my own teenage daughter pulled a stunt like that.

Yet Aunt Emma's independent streak has served her well. When she was diagnosed with breast cancer in her early thirties, having by then acquired a husband and three little girls to care for, she determined to get well. And she did. Though she endured a sloppy surgery that left her with a paralyzed, chronically swollen left arm and hand, as well as an angry chest wound that refused and refused again to heal properly, life for Aunt Emma went on.

Losing her breast, knowing she had cancer, has been traumatic, awful, but it is the loss of the use of her arm that has caused Aunt Emma the most frustrating day-to-day difficulties.

Try fixing a five-year-old's ponytail with one hand, she would challenge. Try chopping a tomato for salad or hanging out a load of laundry or picking a knot out of a wet shoestring.

Try enduring thirty years of strangers asking, "What happened to your arm?"

"I got hit by a car," she would say.

"My husband beat me up," she would deadpan.

"I was at the zoo and a bear got loose," she would lie.

And on bad days, when she could simply take it *no more,* "I have cancer, if it's any of your business!"

And as far as Aunt Emma was concerned, it was no one's business.

I can remember only a handful of times when Aunt Emma discussed her bout with cancer with me. Though we are close, in regards to her body and her emotions about it, she was, and is today, a private person.

After more than three decades of cancer-free good health, I hope that her fear of death from the disease has faded. But I wonder, does it ever? Aunt Emma appears to feel good, and she has adjusted incredibly well to having only one functioning arm—a fact attested to by the fresh peach cobblers she bakes, the family photos she shoots, the collection of throw pillows she sewed for my living room sofa.

Only once do I remember witnessing Aunt Emma's feelings about her cancer spill out unchecked.

Aunt Emma is visiting at my house and we are out running errands together. She tags along with me to pick up my paycheck at the hospital where I am working and rather than wait for me in the hot car, comes in and seats herself on a comfortable couch near the surgical waiting room. I go upstairs to retrieve my check. Janice, the hospital's payroll secretary, is involved in a lengthy phone conversation so my mission takes a few minutes longer than I expect. But finally I get my check and I take the elevator back down.

Aunt Emma is not where I left her. So I look around and quickly spot her sitting near a callous-handed, trembling, and sobbing elderly man. He is a farmer—it is easy to tell, dressed in a pressed khaki shirt and soft, clean overalls.

I watch as a doctor, still clad in surgical scrubs, walks slump shouldered and weary away from the man, back toward the surgical suite from where he came. I hear the rustling sound his shoe covers make with each step he takes.

I watch Aunt Emma and the old man but I say nothing.

"Son! Did you hear what the doctor said?" He speaks to a younger man at his side. "Your mother has cancer. He said they found cancer." His voice shakes and he wrings his hands. "Cancer!"

The younger man tries to keep his composure. Tries to soothe his dad. "She'll be all right, Dad. Mom'll be okay." I hear his voice crack.

"Cancer." The old man shakes his head, pulls a bandana from his pocket and wipes his eyes.

Aunt Emma leans toward the man. "Excuse me, sir. I didn't mean to eavesdrop, but I heard what the doctor told you."

He looks up at her but I'm not sure he *sees* her.

She puts her hand on his arm. "Look at me. I had cancer too. Thirty years ago and I'm fine. I'm just fine. Really."

The man clutches Aunt Emma's hand, latches onto her words. "Did you hear that son? She had cancer and she's still alive. Oh lady, tell me what hospital you went to. We'll take my wife there! If they helped you maybe they can help her."

Aunt Emma stays with the man a few more minutes, speaks softly to him and to his son. Then she stands up, straightens her skirt, clears her throat, and looks at me. "Ready?" she asks.

I nod.

In the car, Aunt Emma buckles her seatbelt, sets her purse on the floor, draws a long breath.

I wait.

She stares out the window for more than a moment. Finally, when she is ready, she says, "People do survive, you know."

"I know," I say.

❧ ❧

And so this afternoon, as I wait by the telephone to find out if this lump in my own breast is a big nothing or a big *something*, as I sip a cup of tea and try not to cry, try for the sake of my husband not to *totally lose it*, I remember her words and I am comforted.

"People do survive," I hear her say.

"I know, Aunt Emma," is my reply. "I know."

"O God, please heal her!"
NUMBERS 12:13

CHAPTER TEN

Angel Soft

*I*t has been almost two years since my sister-in-law Martha phoned me with these shocking words: "I ran into Becky Freeman today in the frozen food section at Super Wal-Mart."

"Becky Freeman? You *know* her?"

"Uh huh. Her kids go to the same school where our boys go. Anyway, we were talking about our husbands and the holidays and about who's supposed to host the next Cub Scout meeting." Martha paused.

"Then I asked her when her next book is coming out, and she said in May, and you know what? She told me that she's also working as an agent or an editor or something like that. So I sort of mentioned that I had a sister-in-law who was a writer and she said you should call her."

"What?"

"She said you should call her."

"But," I squirmed, "Becky Freeman is, you know, a *real* writer. She's written like *five* books."

"But she's really nice," Martha countered. "Call her."

I didn't. Couldn't bring myself to. But, since Martha had given me Becky's address, I *did* write her a fan letter. Told her how much I loved her books and admired her work. In the letter I gave her a little information about myself. And though I felt foolish doing so, I also enclosed copies of a couple of the articles I'd had published in a small Christian magazine.

Two weeks later she called me.

Becky Freeman, Real Writer, called me.

At my house!

Martha was right. Becky *was* nice. She liked my writing and thought I could do a book. I wasn't sure what an agent *was,* but she offered to be mine. And thanks to her prodding and instructing, her encouraging and informing, I did write and see published, my first book, *The Whispers of Angels.*

What fun I've had this past year. Because of the book, I've met interesting people, traveled a bit, been on radio and television, and even received fan mail of my own. And yet when folks who don't know me start to gush a little too much, I remind them, and myself, that even though I've written a book, *a really good book,* I'm still the person at my house who scrubs the toilets and thaws the chickens.

I've had much to learn about how the publishing business works. For while the company interested in producing my book liked my writing, before they would commit to publication, I had to answer a few questions. *Was I willing to do media interviews?* and *Would I be available for book signings and promotional appearances?*

Was I?

Would I?

I couldn't wait.

So when a local bookstore owner asked me to do my first book signing, I eagerly accepted, worried over what to wear, and arrived thirty minutes early.

I was prepared.

So was the store owner.

She had purchased a corsage for me to wear and prepared a lovely place for me to sit and sign. A lace-draped table, flanked by a pair of ceramic angels, supported a white feather pen and held stacks and stacks of my just-released book. Crystal bowls held nuts and mints to go with the coffee and punch she'd made. The owner even provided pink scalloped party napkins, printed with *The Whispers of Angels, Annette Smith,* in silver script.

The signing was lovely. New friends and old stopped by the shop and I signed about fifty copies of my book. But, while folks did a lot of chatting and browsing and shopping, they did little eating. In fact, at the end of the signing, almost all of the nuts and mints remained. Little of the punch had been sipped and only a few cups of coffee dispensed. I doubt more than half a dozen of the pretty napkins were taken.

So when the signing was over, the shop owner gave me some of the nuts and mints and all of the leftover napkins to take home with me. After all, what use did she have for two hundred napkins printed with *my* name?

Once home, I tucked a pair of the napkins away in a drawer—pink scalloped souvenirs of my very first signing. The rest I placed in the kitchen for the family to use for meals and snacks.

They were impressed.

It was not long after the signing that I found myself at home alone on a cold and rainy morning. Since we were out of just about everything, I had planned to use the day to run errands and grocery shop. But after staring out at the miserable weather and foraging through the cupboard, I decided the family could survive one more day without me going to the store. It would take some creative cooking to put together our evening meal, but it was worth it not to get out on such a dreary day. So enjoying my warm and cozy house, I hunkered down with a mug of hot coffee and a chapter idea.

It was not until midmorning that I realized we were out of an item of great importance to the smooth functioning of any busy household. Not only were we out of milk and eggs and bread and laundry soap, we were out of *toilet paper*.

Not low on.

Totally out of.

Not a big problem.

I went to the kitchen, grabbed a bundle of pink scalloped napkins and placed a nice-sized stack neatly on the back of both of the family toilets. Paper is paper—right? I found that for me, the napkins worked just fine.

Not so for my husband.

When he arrived home from work that evening, tired from a long day, stiff from his hour-long commute, he—just as he does every evening—gave me a quick kiss, asked about my day, picked up the newspaper, and headed for the reading . . . I mean the *bath*room.

Within seconds he came bolting back to the kitchen.

"Are we out of toilet paper?" he asked.

"Uh huh," I answered, not looking up from the sauce I was stirring. "Look on the back of the toilet. I put some napkins there. They'll do for now and I'll get some toilet paper in the morning."

Randy leaned against the counter. Shifted uncomfortably. "You put your special napkins in the bathroom to use for . . . " His voice trailed off and a pained expression came across his face. "Your *Whispers of Angels* napkins? You put them in the *bathroom?*"

I shrugged.

He put on his coat.

"Going out?" I questioned, surprised. It was late. Dinner was almost ready.

"To the store. Back in a few minutes."

"Well, okay. Hurry back."

My husband snores when he sleeps, leaves dirty dishes in the den, and rarely notices when I've cut my hair. I'd like for him to talk to me some more, spend Saturdays doing chores, and stop watching sports on TV.

He is a flawed man.

Not so my friend Ashley's husband. My suspicion is that John is perfect. He's handsome, helpful, and a brilliant conversationalist. What more could any wife want? Even Ashley struggles to come up with a complaint about John.

Would I trade?

Randy for John?

Never.

For talk is nice, good looks are great, and I could certainly use more help around the house. But nothing, nothing, compares to a man who, at the end of a long tiring day, puts on his coat and goes back out to buy toilet paper. You've just got to love a man who *refuses* to use *Whispers of Angels* napkins for . . .

I think I'll keep him.

Your desire will be for your husband.
Genesis 3:16

CHAPTER ELEVEN

Little Girl Dreams

y thirteen-year-old daughter received some surprising tests results today. An informal quiz, given at school and de-signed to reflect a student's aptitude for certain career paths, suggests that my sweet-faced daughter consider preparing herself for one of three possible positions: a disc jockey, a uni-versity president, or a bartender.

I suppose I should be pleased to learn that she possesses such diverse talents and abilities!

After discussing with Rachel the inappropriateness of at least *one* of those jobs, I questioned her about what she *does* want to do in the future. After all, in a few short years, she, like her older brother will be finishing high school and preparing for college.

"Have you thought about becoming a teacher," I asked, "like Grandmother, Aunt Diana, and Aunt Martha?"

"I don't think I want to be a teacher."

"How about becoming a nurse like me?"

"Mom, you know I hate blood and stuff."

"You love to shop. I bet you'd be a great saleswoman."

"Maybe."

Rachel folded the test and shoved it back into her backpack. She nibbled on a cookie and sipped from a tumbler of juice. Then, eyes dark and thoughtful, she spoke. "You know Mom, I'm sure I'll go to college and I'll end up being *something,* but what I really want to do is get married and have a bunch of babies and stay at home and take care of them. More than anything in the world, I want to be a mother."

Rachel's words make me smile. Okay, they make my heart *melt.* For while I expect her go to college and though I believe it is important for a young woman to be prepared to support herself, I pray that God will give Rachel the desires of her heart. I think she will be a great mom.

Like Rachel, I always wanted to be a mother. As a young girl, I longed not for nursing positions or book contracts, but for children. In my musings they were named, dressed, rocked, and fed. Like Rachel, babies were what I wanted more than anything else in the whole world.

And when Randy and I married, babies came.

But all did not go according to plan.

Like many young women, I had expected not only to be blessed with perfect children, but to be the perfect mother. And while my real children were even sweeter and smarter and cuter than my imaginary offspring, I was dismayed to find that the older they grew, the more I failed at being the ideal mother I'd always expected to be.

In my dreams, I was always patient, understanding, and kind.

In reality, I was *sometimes* patient, understanding, and kind. *Other* times I was irritable, critical, tired, and cranky. Never, ever, was I as good a mother as I wanted to be.

When Rachel was five and Russell was ten, we made the decision to become foster parents. I suppose I was convinced that, though I had failed in my quest to be the model mother to my own children, I would succeed as a picture-perfect foster mother. I expected that any homeless child, no matter how unhappy, disturbed, or damaged, would be simply transformed by my mother love.

That delusion ended about ten minutes after the arrival of Vicki, our first placement.

Five years old, she arrived not crying and needing a cuddle, but loud and ready to take charge. Of everything. Meals, clothing, toys, and bedtime—Vicki knew exactly how things should operate around the Smith house.

Her way.

She bossed Russell and Rachel around, stood toe-to-toe with Randy when he corrected her, and seemed to delight in hurting my feelings.

"This is gross!" she would exclaim about a special meal I prepared with her in mind.

"I hate this dress," she'd say about an adorable outfit I sewed for her.

"My *real* mother is *lots* prettier than you!" she told me at least once a day.

When Vicki wasn't stomping on my ego at home, she was embarrassing me in public. At the grocery store: Hopping on one foot, waving her arms like a bird, and speaking in a high-pitched, piercing voice, "Mama (she only called me "Mama" when we were out together—at home it was "Annette"), are you *sure* you have enough food stamps?" (Our family has never received food stamps.)

Louder still, at the grocery store, after knocking over a display rack of plastic-wrapped panty hose: "Mama, why aren't you smoking? Don't they let you smoke in this store?" (I've never smoked. Though I thought about starting.)

And while we waited in line to check out: "Mama, why don't people in this family kiss on the mouth? Don't you ever kiss Randy on the mouth?" (Occasionally!)

❧ ❧

Possessing a mind and a spirit all her own, Vicki was not the grateful, loving, easily-won-over orphan I'd expected. Likewise I did not turn out to be the always-compassionate, all-understanding, perfect answer to a little girl's prayers.

Vicki spent only one summer with us before returning to her *real* mother. (The one so much prettier than me.) As I remember that season, I wish I was certain that the time Vicki spent in our home gave her something to take with her, something to hold onto. How I would like to be sure that Vicki left our home better, stronger, more stable than when she came. It would mean so much to know that our family made a lasting, positive impression on her life.

But since I am not privy to the end of Vicki's life story, I can't know and I am left to hope and wonder.

In spite of my doubts, in spite of all the ways I find myself lacking, one thing that I am confident of, one thing that I am sure of: While a loud, wiry, disruptive, and difficult little girl shared our home and our hearts, she was scrubbed and scolded, tucked in and tickled, hugged and held.

Even when she and I were at our worst, Vicki was loved.

While over and over I've blown it as both a mother to my own children and as a make-do mother to foster children, one thing I've done right.

I have loved.

I believe that counts for something.

Love covers over all wrongs.
Proverbs 10:12

CHAPTER TWELVE

Wonder Woman

*S*ara is a city girl. She effortlessly maneuvers her stylish sport utility vehicle down the most congested freeways, bargain hunts at exclusive downtown boutiques, and lunches with friends at trendy, out-of-the-way restaurants. Model thin and blessed with fair skin and shiny black hair, she looks stunning in the dresses and stylish pantsuits she prefers to wear even on weekends. Her current favorite *casual* footwear is a pair of black, high-heel, lace-up suede boots she bought on sale last fall.

I remain unconvinced when she insists, "They really are comfortable, Annette. Try them on."

When my family and I moved from a mid-sized urban area to our present community in the country (population 1,106), I felt instantly at home. There is no doubt, I was meant for rural life. Jeans and T-shirts flatter my figure, and both summer and winter I wear clunky leather sandals that cause my teenagers great good-natured embarrassment. Plowing down dirt roads in my ancient Chevy Suburban in search of a pick-your-own berry farm or an out-of-the-way junk store is my idea of a perfect afternoon. Meeting friends at

Dairy Queen for M&M Blizzards after a ball game is, for me, a much-anticipated outing.

Don't misunderstand; I think the city is a *great* place to *visit*. When I stay with Sara and her family, she treats me to urban experiences she knows I love. We visit art museums, stroll the arboretum, and shop at sprawling, well-stocked bookstores. We feast on fresh croissants each morning and dip crisp almond cookies into cups of strong and steaming gourmet coffee every afternoon. When I leave Sara's house, it is always with the feeling I've been valued and cared for, pampered and spoiled.

But while I relish the culture available in Sara's city, I'm repelled when I watch how she carefully activates her home's security system each time we venture out. For though she and her family reside in a lovely, quiet neighborhood, urban crime is a constant fear and the expensive alarm is a necessity. I wouldn't want to live like that.

When Sara comes to our house, I throw the windows of the guest room wide open to the pine-scented outside air. I layer the bed with crisp cotton sheets and place a bouquet of just-plucked wildflowers on the nightstand. I try to provide her with everything she needs to relax and enjoy the visit: tissues, magazines, snacks, and a bottle of water—everything but an alarm clock. I trust that the rowdy choir practice our resident family of enthusiastic songbirds holds each daybreak will wake her early each morning.

When I host Sara, we munch banana-nut muffins on the deck and take lazy afternoon strolls in the forest. Our time together is peaceful, calm, and quietly laid-back. I am confident she enjoys our visits, but I suspect at the same time Sara is made just a bit restless by the snail's pace of our country community. While she respects, and even understands the life we've chosen, I believe she mourns the lack of stimulating activities available to me and my family.

Sara had yet to meet her husband Dale when his brother and I were married. We were wed in a simple ceremony, joined beneath an oak tree in my parents' backyard. When the time came, I marched right down the mown grass aisle toward my life as a married woman. Waiting on my left was a teenage bridesmaid, dressed in white platform sandals and a long ruffled peasant dress. Buttoned into a new, baby blue polyester suit, Randy stood on the right. After the short ceremony, our guests nibbled on cake and peanuts served from a table draped with a yellow-checked cloth. Glad-it-was-over children wrestled on the grass with half a dozen curious neighborhood dogs.

It was the wedding I'd always dreamed of. Perfect.

I was present a few years later when Sara and Dale were married in a moving ceremony held in the lovely sunroom of a high-rise hotel. Elegant and sleek in her designer gown, Sara stepped gracefully down the aisle to classical music played by a professional harpist. Tall, dark, and handsome, Dale looked perfectly at ease in his owned (not rented) tuxedo. At the reception, bow-tied waiters served delicious gourmet hors d'oeuvres from silver and crystal serving trays.

Sara and Dale's wedding was both festive and formal. And it was exactly the wedding they'd hoped for and planned on.

She and I have grown and changed in the years since we became sisters-in-law. Though outsiders would comment that our husbands married startlingly different women, we are in fact, crazy about each other.

Rearing a daughter in the 90s is a difficult task. With today's rising divorce rate and heart-wrenching reports of increasing domestic violence, teaching a daughter to expect a Cinderella-like future is both irresponsible and unwise. Though I hope for, and in fact expect, Rachel to enjoy what I have—a loving husband and a stable home—I believe it is my task to instill in her a healthy sense of independence, to teach her self-reliance and accountability. I never want Rachel to feel she has no choices, or to believe she must remain trapped in an unsafe domestic situation.

When I discuss child-rearing with my peers, I find my concerns are universally shared by other women who mother girls. A recent phone call from Sara turned, as it usually does, to our children, this time to her articulate six-year-old daughter.

"I'm worried about Allie," Sara told me.

"Allie?" I asked. "What's the matter?"

"She is watching entirely too much television. And she's hooked on old reruns. You know—from the sixties."

Leave it to Beaver . . . Mr. Ed . . . Gilligan's Island . . . I mused. *Those shows are a lot more wholesome than so much of the trash that's on these days.*

"It's not just *any* of the old shows she likes." Sara interrupted my thoughts. "The only two she cares to watch, over and over, are 'I Dream of Jeannie' and 'Bewitched.' Allie is just *mesmerized* by their leading female characters. Remember those two?"

I did remember. My elementary school friends and I passed our time on the playground trying to wriggle our noses like the conniving wife Samantha on "Bewitched." The Christmas my cousins Carolyn and Sharon and I were about Allie's age, we received matching pairs of diaphanous, pastel-striped harem pajamas. Their scratchy nylon fabric itched us terribly but we loved them anyway. We three girls spent the entire holiday perfecting Jeannie's coy head-bob as we chanted, "Yes master, your wish is my command."

"What are you going to do? What did you tell her?" I queried.

"I sat Allie down and told her it was fine for her to watch her favorite TV shows occasionally, but I wanted her to realize the female characters were not good role models. I explained that a wife should be honest with her husband and not try to trick him into doing things or hide things from him like Samantha. I tried to let her know it is not appropriate to dress up in skimpy clothing and call a man 'master' like Jeannie."

"Good for you, Sara. Did you get through?"

"Not exactly." Sara sounded chagrinned. "When I finished my little speech, I asked Allie if she understood. Do you know how she responded?"

"How?"

"Her exact words were: 'But Mom, I like to watch those shows because *the women have the power!*' "

Almost a year ago, Randy and Dale's Uncle James became very ill. He was hospitalized, two hours from his home, in the city where Dale and Sara live. His illness, from which, sadly, he would not recover, stretched from an anticipated few days into a two-month-long bedside marathon for his devoted wife Edna. Worried and heartsick, she insisted on staying with him at the hospital rather than returning to her home.

From the first day of James' illness, Dale and Sara did what they could to help Edna. They called, visited, brought her fresh clothing, and occasionally convinced her to leave the hospital for a hasty lunch.

Early in her husband's illness, Edna, a strong and independent wife, appeared unfazed by her tiring vigil. But as James' stay in the hospital stretched on and on, she began to look more and more exhausted. It was feared that Edna might be approaching her breaking point. Extremely concerned, Dale and Sara tried to convince her to come and stay at their house, to at least get some sleep and a hot bath.

Adamantly, she declined. "I'm fine. Just fine. And I'm getting *plenty* of rest on the waiting room couch. Don't worry about me."

Edna refused to leave the hospital and no one was able to convince her otherwise.

Except Sara.

A surprised Dale, two days later, arrived home to find his living room transformed into a spa—a place designed for relaxation and pampering. Edna, wrapped in Sara's own white terry robe, rested on the sofa, feet elevated on a down pillow, face partially obscured by a lavender-scented eye pillow. Her hands rested limply at her sides. Kneeling near the end of the couch, Sara quickly motioned for Dale to keep his voice down, but never paused from the gentle foot massage she was giving Edna.

Sara had spared no luxurious detail. A dozen vanilla candles provided the room's only illumination while Pachelbel's "Canon in D" lilted from the CD player. A china cup of herbal tea flanked by two gourmet pecan cookies sat ready for snacking on the coffee table.

Dale grinned. "How," he whispered, "did you *ever* get her to come?"

Before Sara could answer, Edna let out a loud, long, nasal snore. They held their sides to keep from giggling.

Dale repeated his whisper. "How did you talk her into coming over?"

Sara shrugged. "This morning I went to the hospital to check on her and to see how James was doing. They'd had a rough time of it last night and Edna was so tired she could hardly stand. I didn't exactly ask if she wanted to come over. It was more like I *told* her she was taking a break and that was the end of it. I picked up her purse and I put her coat over her shoulders and I took her by the hand. I told the nurses where she would be and asked them to call if James' condition changed. And you know what? She didn't even put up a protest."

Dale shook his head at the mental picture of his soft-spoken wife ordering strong-willed Aunt Edna around like a child. Telling her what to do. And getting away with it!

His thoughts were interrupted abruptly when, without warning, sound-sleeping, completely-at-ease Edna heaved yet another great, much-needed, sighing snore.

❧ ❧

I believe that my niece is right. Some women *do* have all the power. And though loving and tending and nurturing and caring aren't nearly as impressive to watch as feminine television magic, they *are* powerful just the same.

If there be any doubt, just ask Edna.

When she wakes up.

He gives strength to the weary
And increases the power of the weak.
Isaiah 40:29

CHAPTER THIRTEEN

Sister to Sister

When I was five years old, I asked my mom and my dad, Santa Claus, the Easter bunny, God, and Jesus to send me a baby sister. It wasn't that I didn't love my toddler twin brothers, I just wished for, longed for, *dreamed* of having a female sibling.

I was positive that if I got one, if *anyone* could arrange for me to have one, my sister and I would be best friends forever.

But tragically, *no one* did and I was forced to grow up alone, just my two brothers and me.

When I was eighteen I met my husband-to-be, Randy. We dated and fell in love and in time I was taken to meet his mother and his daddy and his younger brother, Dale. They were friendly and nice and I liked them just fine. But it was not until I met his brown-eyed little sister, Diana, that I knew for certain these were the in-laws for me.

Diana, like me, had two brothers. She, also like me, had always wanted a sister.

When Randy and I married, Diana was my bridesmaid. When Russell was born, she drove three hours to see him. When she and her husband, Bruce, were wed a year later, I stood beside her in a lavender taffeta dress and dyed-to-match pumps with inch and a half heels. Two years after that, when their first son, Stewart, was born, I went as soon as I heard.

During the early years of our marriage, I can't count how many times she and Bruce showed up with a pickup truck and a dolly to help us move. As young brides, Diana and I shared recipes and baby pictures and once I sewed her a blue-striped maternity dress.

This year I'm almost forty and Diana's but a few years behind me. We find ourselves commiserating about our teenagers and talking about our careers and wondering how to best cover the gray hairs we suddenly find too numerous to keep plucking.

I love all my sisters-in-law: My own brothers' wives, Dale and Martha, and Randy's brother's wife, Sara. Really, I love them all the same. But unlike Diana and me, none of them are the only girls in their families. I don't think they can understand what it has been like for Diana and me to grow up without sisters, and to long for one, and to be so happy to finally be granted one.

Diana is doubly blessed. She shares that sisterless bond not just with me, but also with her husband's blond-haired, only sibling, Karen. The two of them live in the same town. Have for many of their married years, and they are crazy about each other.

Karen called Diana when she learned she was pregnant.

Diana called Karen when she learned *she* was pregnant.

Karen called Diana when she learned that her baby was in trouble.

And when a tiny little girl, a child born too young to live, was taken from Karen's arms, Diana stood in the hall and wept.

In the hours after the baby's doomed delivery, Karen, though physically all right, appeared almost out of her mind with shock and grief. Trembling and shaking, her body went from cold to hot to cold again, her head pounded and her stomach knotted. Her breath came hard. Even though she'd not slept in more than two days, she couldn't close her eyes. Just couldn't.

"You need to rest," her worried mother told her.

"I can give you a sleeping pill," a helpful nurse offered.

"Try to sleep," her weary husband urged.

But Karen shook her head and clutched at the covers and refused to close her eyes.

Finally, Diana eased the rest of the family from Karen's room. "Go get some coffee, some lunch. I'll stay with her. Go."

Reluctantly, but obediently, they did.

The two of them alone, Diana brushed Karen's hair and washed Karen's face, straightened her sheets, and sat down beside her. "Karen," she said firmly, "I want you to go to sleep now."

Karen shook her head.

"What's wrong? Are you in pain?" Diana questioned.

"No."

"Then what is it? Tell me."

"I'm afraid."

"Afraid? Of what?"

Fresh tears. "I'm afraid that if I close my eyes I might never, ever open them again. I feel like I'm going to die."

Diana wiped away tears of her own. Moved her chair up close and put her face next to Karen's. "Tell you what. I'll stay right here. Right here beside you. I'll hold your hand and I'll watch your face and I'll feel for your breath and if you start to die, I'll just wake you up. Okay?"

No answer.

"Okay, Karen?"

"Okay."

And so at last, with Diana right there, Karen was able to relax. And Diana kept her word. For hours she sat next to Karen and kept watch while she slept. Her legs went numb and her neck got stiff and she was urged to get up, to let someone else have a turn.

But she didn't. Wouldn't.

Karen went on to have another child (a fine son), to suffer through and heal from a sad divorce, and to marry again to a good strong man. And when she learned, early in her second marriage, that she was unexpectedly, delightfully, how-did-this-happen pregnant again, Diana was among those she called first.

And though this pregnancy has been a scary one, a stay-in-bed-and-pray-for-just-one-more-day kind of ordeal, today, with the pregnancy at thirty-four weeks, the doctors are smiling and nodding and saying the odds look good.

"And," they tell Karen, "it will be a girl."

And when this baby is born, Diana will once again be there for Karen. She'll rub her back and she'll tell her she's fine, and if Karen is scared she'll sit right beside her and keep watch while she sleeps.

And when someone who doesn't really know Diana comments on her devotion and her love for someone who's not even related by blood, Diana will hold her tongue. She'll smile and shrug and answer calmly, "That's what sisters do."

And Diana will be right.

For whether we are related by blood or love or both, that is what sisters do.

You are my sister.
PROVERBS 7:4

CHAPTER FOURTEEN

Romance Is in the Bag

The first thing I did after my husband proposed to me (well, the second thing—the first thing was to say yes) was shoo him home so that I could rush to the closest drugstore newsstand and purchase a copy of *Brides* magazine.

I had been waiting twenty years for this moment.

I've known folks without saddles who subscribe to *Western Horseman* and I've met jelly-bellied couch potatoes who save all the back issues of *Muscle and Fitness*. I even have one friend who can't boil an egg, yet she wouldn't dream of missing an issue of *Bon Appétit*.

But, when it comes to *Brides,* there is an unbreakable, premarital, periodical code. No woman—I mean *no* woman—buys *Brides* magazine until she has a engagement ring on her finger and a date in mind.

And so on that December evening almost twenty years ago, I proudly slid the hefty magazine across the counter, flashed my new diamond ring, and paid my three dollars. I couldn't wait to get the book home, call my girlfriends to come over (for it is considered *perfectly fine* to look at someone else's *Brides* before you're engaged, you just can't buy it for yourself), and study it page by page.

And that's what I did. The glossy marital magazine was crammed full of helpful articles and beautifully done ads. I picked out my wedding dress, gleaned ideas for the flowers, clipped coupons for invitations, and memorized a thirty-eight item checklist titled "How to Have a Perfect Wedding." I chose china and stoneware and flatware and silver and I sent off for free pamphlets that would bring detailed descriptions of exotic, out-of-budget honeymoon destinations right to my mailbox.

And I dreamed. Of my romance-filled life with my handsome husband. I planned how we would share candlelit dinners and intimate breakfasts at dawn, moonlit strolls and heart-to-heart talks. My sweetie and I would enjoy every minute of our new life together. I was sure that just like the white-toothed couples between the covers of the magazine, we would we would always be smiling and beautiful and happy together.

Six months later, our outdoor wedding was indeed lovely, and our budget honeymoon memorable. I can proudly say that both lived up to all of my dreams. Actually, it was not until we had settled into our first married couple apartment that things didn't go according to plan.

My plan.

First of all, Randy didn't eat breakfast. Ever. *And* he didn't talk unnecessarily before 10 A.M. As for candlelit dinners, my new husband preferred to *see* what he was eating (not a bad idea considering what an inexperienced cook I was), and he favored drinking his iced tea from a plastic NFL-decaled tumbler instead of from a crystal wedding goblet.

Randy liked to run, not stroll. He enjoyed movies with car chases and shootings more than concerts in the park, bologna more than fruited chicken salad, pot pies more than pâté. His idea of dress for a casual night out together was sweatpants and sneakers with no socks. Mine was sandals, pearls, and a gauzy sundress. He wanted to spend Saturday afternoons playing basketball with his buddies. I wanted to spend it strolling art museums. With him.

And while none of the smiling couples in *Brides* looked like they *ever* suffered from an odor problem, we both woke up with terrible morning breath.

This was *not* the marriage I'd thought I would have. Feeling disappointed and neglected, even sometimes un-loved, I picked fights.

"You never want to spend time with me," I whined.

"Yes I do."

"No you don't."

"I do too."

"When?"

"I'm with you now, aren't I?"

"That's not what I mean!"

And so on. I dreamed of closeness as the joined-at-the hip variety. Randy expected a casual companion.

I longed for romantic days. Randy craved romance of the nocturnal variety.

During one particularly memorable argument, I remember backing him into a verbal corner with repeated, nonsensi-cal, for-which-there-are-no-answers questions. "Just why do you even *want* to be married?" I demanded. "What do you even *like* about being married?"

"I don't know," my sweet husband shrugged, "I guess I just like having someplace to go when I get off work."

Not the reply I'd had in mind.

About ten years into our union (which *did* survive that first year, and has somehow even managed to thrive during the almost two decades we've been together), Randy and his fellow coach, Richard, attended a spring-time, seven-day, out-of town, coaches' convention. The two guys spent the week attending various clinics related to the respective sports they teach. They walked through exhibit halls, picked up free samples, and haggled with sales reps over prices for next year's team uniforms. They listened to motivational speakers, watched training videos . . . and they played a lot of golf.

While Randy was gone, I busily prepared for a trip of my own. Several months before, I had been asked to participate in a two-week, medical evangelistic campaign to Ivory Coast, Africa.

Africa.

Me.

I couldn't believe it!

I was so excited when I found out I was going, that at first I told everyone I knew. But while *some* folks *did* share my enthusiasm, the reactions of other people startled and stung.

"How can you leave your children?"

"You're going to Africa?"

"Without your husband?"

"For two weeks?"

"*Without your husband?*"

And so I began to wonder. To squirm. *Was I a bad wife? Would my children be damaged by my absence? Should I stay home?*

These thoughts were racing around in my head and heart when Randy arrived home from his trip. I was eager to talk to him, to ask, *Should I forget about going to Africa? Do you want me to stay home? Is it wrong for me to leave both you and the kids?* But Russell and Rachel were excited to see him, wanted to sit on him and talk to him, and he was tired and ready to rest. And so I hugged him and I kissed him and I cooked his favorite meal and I held my tongue until later.

Once the kids were in bed, Randy spoke, "I brought you a present."

"A present? What for?"

He looked a bit embarrassed. "Richard wanted to bring his wife something so I thought I'd get you something too."

"Oh."

"Richard bought his wife a bottle of perfume."

"How nice."

"But I knew you already had some perfume, so I got you something else. It's not exactly what you'd call a romantic gift," he told me. "I bought you something you can use."

Not exactly words to make a wife's heart pound in anticipation.

"I got you a suitcase."

Brand new. Navy blue.

"You're going to need it."

Wheels and a pull strap. Lots of zippers and a combination lock.

"For your trip."

Randy is a smart man. He is almost always right about almost everything. But that time Randy was wrong. I wrapped my arms around him and I told him that the suitcase *was* a romantic gift. Since that time, Randy has gifted me with perfume and flowers and even some jewelry, but that new suitcase remains today, in my mind, the most romantic gift he has ever given me.

🌿

Next Saturday I'll board an airplane to go on yet another trip. This time I'm traveling to Mexico, where I'll spend my days working among some of the poorest of the poor. And when the week is over and when I step off the plane, once again back home in Texas, Randy will be there waiting for me.

He always is.

He'll load my bag into the car and he'll take me out to dinner and then he'll turn that car in the direction of our house. And when we pull into the driveway, I'll see that he's left the porch light on and I'll remember those words he spoke when we were young newlyweds.

And I'll know Randy was right *then* and that he is right *now.*

The best thing, the very best thing about being married, is that once you are married, you always, *always,* have someplace to go after work.

I don't believe it gets any better.

I will surely return to you.
GENESIS 18:10

CHAPTER FIFTEEN

Nap Time
with The Screamer

I have always had a way with words. When my four-years-younger-than-me brothers and I were growing up, I could talk them into doing almost anything. Under my sisterly direction, the two of them jumped off of dangerously high stacks of loosely baled hay, crossed fast-rising, storm-swollen creeks, and used my jump rope to tie their bicycles to the back bumpers of cranked-up motor vehicles.

It is a wonder my brothers survived their childhoods and I am grateful for their forgiving natures.

Now grown up, Bruce, the oldest of the twins, is a doctor. He and his wife and two baby girls live in Appalachia, where he takes care of the poor.

Dayne, the quieter of my two brothers, works as an engineer for an international company near a large metropolitan area. He and his wife—a curly-haired girl he fell in love with before he reached his thirteenth birthday—have two sons.

Being a nurse, I am able to understand Bruce's love for his work, can share the passion he feels about the medical profession. When he tells me about his practice or describes an interesting case to me, I listen with rapt attention.

But I confess. Though I am proud of him and love him dearly, I am basically clueless as to what Dayne does when he goes to work. I know that he loves his job and that at an almost unheard-of young age he has risen through the ranks to hold a position of leadership, authority, and accountability. His role in the company is one that brings with it many rewards, but also great amounts of stress. Unfortunately, for the next few years Dayne's job will require him to travel from home a good part of every week.

Our lives are very different.

Dayne's wife, Martha, came to him from a family of four girls. When she married Dayne, her three sisters claimed him as their own, for they all thought it would be wonderful to have a brother. And it was. They think that Dayne is a *great* brother.

He is there for them.

On a recent fall evening, Martha received sad word that the husband of dear Mrs. Johnson, her dad's secretary and friend for many years, had passed away. Martha's parents were out of town and were distressed that it would be impossible for them to make it home in time to go to the funeral. So Martha called her youngest sister, Judy, the sibling who lives closest, and the two of them stewed over what to do. They both wanted to go, felt the need to go, but the service would take place the very next day in a town more than three hours away.

Dayne, luckily, on the day of the funeral would be enjoying a rare day off at home. Though he had taken vacation hours, in reality he planned to spend the day working off and on, puttering at the computer and spending time returning phone calls. He needed a day to catch up. But since he would be home and therefore available to pick the boys up after school, he urged Martha to go to the funeral.

It was important.

Judy, however, ran into a problem. She was unable to find a sitter for baby Kendall. Though she made call after call, no one she reached was available on such a short notice. Just as Judy was ready to give up, she and Martha impulsively decided to go anyway. Judy and Kendall would sit in the car, or drive around, or do *something* while Martha attended the funeral service. At the graveside, they would take turns. One of them would stay with the baby in the car while the other visited with the family.

"Nonsense," said Dayne when he heard their plan. *He* would be home. He would keep the baby.

Now Kendall is perhaps one of the prettiest babies born. Big liquid eyes, long lashes, soft brown curls—but the little girl is LOUD. Her mom and her dad, her aunts and her uncles, even her grandparents on *both* sides call her The Screamer. It doesn't matter if Kendall is happy or sad, hungry or full, wet or dry—everyone within earshot *is going to hear about it.* She possesses a terrific set of lungs and uses them at top decibel during mealtimes and at bedtime, in the grocery store, at the mall, and when her mother is on the telephone.

Kendall is a non-stop noise machine and is made truly happy only when she is being heard *and* being held.

"No way." Judy, though tempted, wouldn't consider leaving Kendall with Dayne. He deserved some peace, some rest, some quiet, some time to de-stress on his day off. Dayne did *not* need to spend a day with The Screamer.

But Dayne talked to her, convinced her, and assured her that he wanted to do it for them. He wanted to do it for Mrs. Johnson. "Go," he told Judy firmly. "Kendall and I will be fine."

Reluctantly, Judy gave in. And when, after several false starts, she and Martha finally walked out the door, they did so leaving Dayne on a business call to California, holding Kendall in his arms.

Judy, afflicted with the anxiety and guilt *truly* understood only by another mother of a high-maintenance child, helped Martha drive, sat through the funeral, and greeted Mrs. Johnson appropriately at the cemetery. But, inside, she worried all day about how much trouble she was sure Kendall was giving Dayne. She fretted over poor Dayne, on his day of vacation, having to deal with not just any baby, but with The Screamer.

Martha tried to tell Judy to relax, not to worry. She was sure Dayne and Kendall were fine. Dayne was probably enjoying the day.

Judy was doubtful.

At noon, the two of them stopped for lunch. Judy phoned Dayne from the restaurant. Martha watched as her sister dialed the number, fumed and fidgeted, leaned first on one foot and then on the other waiting for the call to go through. It was nap time and Kendall, always preferring to scream rather than sleep, would be giving Dayne fits about now.

Judy had admitted to Martha that yes it *was* nice to eat a meal out in peace, to have uninterrupted adult conversation, and yes she *had* needed a little break, even if it was to go to a funeral. But *still,* she repeated to herself, she should *not* have imposed on Dayne.

Finally, someone picked up the phone.

Judy had not even heard it ring. "Dayne?" she blurted out. "Is everything all right?"

"Sure it is." His voice was nonchalant. "Everything's fine here. Y'all make it to the funeral okay?"

"Uh huh. Did Kendall go to sleep?"

"Yep. She's conked out right now."

"I know she cried a lot. She always does. Dayne, I'm so sorry . . ."

Dayne interrupted. "She didn't cry at all."

"*Kendall?* Didn't cry?" Judy was suspicious. Didn't believe him.

"Nope. When she got tired, she just laid her head down and closed her eyes."

"You just put her in bed?"

"Well, no . . ."

Suddenly Judy figured it out. Held the picture in her mind. Dayne was holding Kendall.

And he was. In fact, Dayne had held the baby *the whole morning*. He had held her while he worked on the computer and held her while he made his business calls. And when Kendall got sleepy, she just put her head down on his shoulder and closed her eyes.

Dayne said not to be in any hurry to get home. He was feeling good.

Judy relaxed and said *she* felt good.

Martha, who loves them both, knew all *was* good.

When hours later Judy and Martha arrived home, they found the house dim and dreamy-quiet. The two of them tiptoed into the den and found Dayne and Kendall asleep on the couch. Kendall was nestled under an afghan, sprawled across Dayne's chest. Their breaths came slowly and it was obvious the two of them were enjoying their heart-to-heart nap.

Sometimes what we think is a sacrifice turns out to be, for someone else, a blessing.

❧ ❧

At this stage of his life, Dayne's days revolve around airports and emails, million dollar budgets, and complicated reports. His world is one that I do not comprehend. But, because I *am* interested in his life, I *want* to hear about what he does, and I seek to understand it.

When I saw him last and asked him, as I always do, what he had been up to lately, Dayne did not speak of his job. Instead, he told me about keeping Kendall while Martha and Judy went to Mr. Johnson's funeral and about what a good day it had been for him. He mentioned what the two of them ate for lunch, and told me about the walk around the yard they took. I learned that Kendall likes mashed potatoes and chocolate pudding and that she loves to listen to the birds.

Days later, I saw Dayne again. He forgot that he'd already told me about his day with Kendall, and so he told me about it again. In great detail. About how what a good day it was.

And because I love him, I listen.

Again.

And as I hear Dayne relate the details of that day, I realize that though there is a large portion of my brother's life that I *don't* comprehend, there is a bigger part of my him that I will always know.

And I think that I have been wrong.

He and I aren't so different after all.

And God saw that it was good.
GENESIS 1:18

CHAPTER SIXTEEN

The Year of Jubilee

I make pancakes for my family's breakfast most every Sunday morning. I've learned for a fact that our family's Sunday morning menu is a tradition not to be messed with.

Over the years there have been times when I've grown weary of the mixing and the pouring, the flipping and the stacking, and so I've tried substituting eggs, biscuits, French toast, even spicy breakfast burritos for our first meal of the week. But each time I've attempted to branch out so boldly, my creative culinary efforts have met with yelps of protest from my husband and my children.

"But we *always* have pancakes on Sunday."

"*Always,* Mom," they remind me.

As if I could forget.

My mother is to blame for this sticky Sunday syrup-and-butter ritual. It didn't begin with me. I am only following her example when I flip those flapjacks. All my growing up years, before we hurried off to Sunday School, my brothers and I, just like my children, feasted on hot-off-the-griddle cakes mom made for us. We loved the ones she made for us then, just as much as my family loves the ones I make for them now.

My mom is a good cook, a creative cook, but most of all, a frugal cook. She did not then and does not now, waste *anything*. Her refrigerator and freezer are crammed full of margarine tubs and canning jars, all of them labeled and containing anywhere from a tablespoon to a half-cup of *perfectly good food*. Food that she or my dad *will eat*.

Someday.

Last week, while visiting my parents, I volunteered to help Mom make dinner. At her request I rummaged through her over-the-fridge freezer compartment—my goal to locate a Baggie of buttered bread crumbs she needed to top a casserole. To my horror, buried between a bag of green beans and a carton of sliced peaches, I found an ice cream container, inscribed in cryptic, black permanent marker block letters—in my mother's handwriting—the word *CAT*.

"Cat?" I looked at her questioningly.

"The neighbor's," she answered absently.

"*Cat?*" I repeated, my eyes widening.

She looked up from the potatoes she was mashing, saw my face, and giggled. "Not *the* neighbor's cat," she explained. "*For* the neighbor's cat. Fish scraps."

The woman wastes *nothing*.

These days, with just herself and my dad to feed, using up leftovers *does* require some inventive efforts. On the same recent visit, after Sunday breakfast, Mom excused herself to get ready for church while Dad and I lingered over our coffee. I got up to rinse my cup, looked out the kitchen window, and saw more than a dozen enormous black birds sitting on the split rail fence that surrounds their yard.

"Look at those birds," I exclaimed. "They are *huge*. I've never seen such big crows."

"They come every Sunday," my dad spoke from behind his paper. "They're waiting for their pancakes."

I must have heard wrong.

"Your mother feeds the crows leftover pancakes every Sunday."

"Pancakes? What do they eat the rest of the week? Bacon and eggs?"

"Don't know. They only come on Sundays. They'll sit on the fence until they get their pancakes. Once they do, they'll fly off. We won't see them again till next week."

Go figure. Only for my mother's Sunday morning pancakes would a host of blackbirds consult a calendar.

By the time most women reach their fiftieth birthday, the year described in the Bible as the "Year of Jubilee," they are ready to slow down a bit.

Not my mom.

When it was announced from the pulpit that the two and three year olds were in desperate need of a Sunday School teacher, in fact, *did not have a teacher at all,* the sensible-shoe-wearing, streaked-with-gray hair set, though scattered in pews all over the sanctuary, ducked behind their hymn books in one perfectly synchronized motion.

They had *been there, done that,* and *did not want to do it again.*

Mom, however, because of her notoriously poor sense of timing, did not duck nearly fast enough. Mom, in fact, allowed herself to be talked into teaching the class. And Dad agreed to help her.

As a twenty-something-year-old Sunday School teacher, Mom might have subscribed to the Sit Down And Be Quiet And Listen To The Bible Story method of teaching. But not so as a woman in her year of jubilee. *These children are just babies,* she thinks. *They need movement, action, can't be expected to sit still.*

And so action and movement are the methods she uses to teach them. When the children studied the Old Testament story of baby Moses hidden in a basket in the Nile River, she filled a washtub full of water and the children floated their own plastic babies in the water. When she taught them about Jesus and the miracle of the loaves and the fishes, she fed them goldfish crackers. And when they learned about Noah and the ark, at her direction, my dad hauled in a rowboat so they could all get inside.

The students, *and their parents,* love my mother's class. And graciously, the Sunday School director asks few questions.

It was during the spring quarter, the time in which the children were to learn about the creation, that Mom got the idea to bring a different stuffed animal to class every week. First a bunny, next a bear, later a puppy. The children could see and feel the critter of the week and while they did so, Mom sang songs about how God made the animals. That went so well that even after the quarter was completed, she continued bringing stuffed animals to class. But what she really wished for was a live animal she could share with her students.

A turtle would be nice, she mused one week. *Turtles don't make noise. They're portable and polite. The children would really enjoy seeing a turtle, could even touch his shell. Maybe I'll find one in the yard or on the road this week.*

But she didn't.

Until, that is, Sunday, when after breakfast, Mom went out to give the crows their pancakes. She almost stepped on—what else?—a turtle. He was perfect. Small and brown, a friendly face, and not too shy. So she picked him up, brought him inside the house, and because she'd heard that reptiles *can* carry disease, she scrubbed him down with antiseptic soap.

Mom's tiny students loved Mr. Turtle. They laughed and clapped their hands and took turns touching his clean shell. Some of them even joined in when she sang, "God made Mr. Turtle."

When class was over, Mom put Mr. Turtle into his shoebox and took him home. Once she was back at the house, she returned to the fence to let him go in the same place where she had found him. Grateful for his freedom and slightly traumatized by his first trip to church, Mr. Turtle quickly disappeared into the grass.

Mom watched him go.

But that was not the end of Mr. Turtle. Mom was *very* surprised when the next Sunday, and the next, and again the next, when she went out to feed the crows, she found him waiting for her by the fence. And since he *just happened* to be there, several weeks in a row, she picked him up, gave him his Sunday morning bath, and took him to church.

He seemed to enjoy it.

I know Mom did.

My mom is a special woman. As she, this year, approaches the end of her fifties, I don't see her as getting any older, just better. I hope I age just like her.

When I make my family's pancakes next Sunday, when later today I paw through my own crowded freezer, and when tomorrow morning I fill the bird feeder (with seed, not pancakes), I will think of my mom and of her year of jubilee.

As I approach my next birthday, my fortieth, I'm thinking that perhaps I'll just skip my fourth decade and go straight to my fifth. Because if *my* fiftieth year is half as much fun as my *mom's* fiftieth year, I can hardly wait.

Happy birthday, Mom!

Consecrate the fiftieth year and proclaim liberty
throughout the land to all its inhabitants.
It shall be a jubilee for you.
LEVITICUS 25:10

CHAPTER SEVENTEEN

Do You Know Our Mother?

*I*t felt good to come out of the stuffy cramped van, to uncurl at last. I'd ridden, the last hundred miles or so, with my feet resting upon someone's sleeping bag, my elbow wedged against someone else's jumbo can of popcorn. Rachel, finding no place else to sit, had wedged herself between the front seats, scrunched down as best she could, uncomplaining, on an ice chest. I knew for a fact that she'd not bent her knees since the last time we'd stopped.

It felt *really* good to get out of that van.

We'd come, all ten members of the mission team, bathed in prayer and accompanied by lots and lots of gear, to this tiny village deep in the heart of central Mexico. We would spend the week with the people and would treat sick bodies, sick souls, sick cows, and sick goats.

But first we would unload. Bags and boxes, crates and containers. Medical supplies to the church building, dental equipment to the school, men to the house on the left, women to one on the right. It took the better part of an hour to get everything situated, and by the time we had done so, a crowd had gathered in the area where we were staying. The gapers included lots and lots of children. The more daring of the kiddos ran up and tugged on our skirts; the shyer ones hid behind their mothers. Preteen boys, trying to appear manly, watched silently from their perches atop a board fence. Their fathers stood to the back and their mamas and grandmas watched us and whispered to each other, hiding their faces behind hand-woven shawls.

The people were not rude to stand and observe us. Just interested. We knew that, and so we smiled at them and talked to them and clumsily groped for the particular Spanish words we needed—words that simply refused to come to our tired, road-weary, English-speaking brains. Once we were unpacked, all of us gave up trying to talk. We simply waved our good nights and went to bed early.

After a night of deep, restful sleep—sleep that was ended abruptly by a dual burro and rooster wake-up call—we all felt better. In the house where we women were staying we stretched and yawned and forced ourselves to come out of warm sleeping bags and get into cool clothes.

Rachel and I, ready for some fresh air and hoping to be first in line at the outhouse, were quick to dress and get going. Together we stumbled over the threshold, squinty-eyed against the bright sunlight. We almost tripped over three well-scrubbed, darling little girls perched on the front stoop of the house.

They stood up quickly. I sensed that the girls had been waiting for us. For a while. Wanted to talk.

"Good morning," we greeted them.

"Good morning," they answered in unison. Their smiles did not dim, but they were suddenly shy. They looked at the ground. The youngest fiddled with her hair.

The owner of the one-room home where we women had spent the night had vacated it for us, was spending the week with a neighbor. Perhaps the little girls lived here, had come to get something they needed, clothing or school books. "Is this your house?" Rachel asked in a friendly voice.

"No," they giggled.

"What are your names?" I asked.

"Ellia."

"Maria."

"Dulce."

"Pretty names. This is my daughter, Rachel. My name is Annette."

More giggles.

Finally, middle sister Maria spoke. "Are you from the United States?"

"Yes."

"From Texas?"

"Yes."

"Our mama is in Texas. Do you know her?"

I looked at Rachel and she looked at me. "Your mama lives in Texas?"

"She works in Dallas. In April, she came to see us and brought us presents. In May, she left so she could work some more. She has to make money but she's coming back soon. She promised."

The month was November. I counted in my head and realized that the girls had not seen their mother in seven months.

"Who takes care of you while your mama's away?" The sisters looked to be less than ten years old, all of them, but they looked well-fed, they were clean and tidy and dressed appropriately for the weather.

"Grandma," answered Ellia. "We live with Grandma." Then she repeated her question. "Have you seen our mama?"

The three little girls looked first me and then at Rachel and then at both of us. Their faces held heartbreaking hope.

My mouth felt like cotton. I was without words. "Texas is a big state and . . ."

Rachel interrupted me. "Is your mama about this tall?" She held up her hand and looked thoughtful.

"Yes!" their eyes widened.

"Does she have brown hair?" Rachel touched her own hair.

"Uh huh," the three girls drew close to her. I eased back from the four of them.

"Are her eyes brown too, and *is* she very, very beautiful?"

All three of their faces were close to hers, holding onto her words. "Yes, she is! She *is* very beautiful! You know her! You know her!"

Rachel looked over their heads, caught my eye. She did not swallow. She did not blink. "I have a message for you from your mama. She loves you very much and she misses you and she thinks about you every single day."

Their eyes shone.

They were happy.

They had received what they had come for.

They gave Rachel a hug and the three of them skipped away, hand in hand, back home to Grandma.

Rachel and I shielded our eyes from the sun and watched them go. We did not speak.

Rachel is barely a teenager, yet already so wise. One of the reasons I bring her with me on mission trips is so that she can learn compassion, so that she can see and learn and be *imprinted* with a lifelong sense of responsibility to care for those less fortunate than her.

I believe she has learned.

And he took the children in his arms,
put his hands on them and blessed them.
MARK 10:16

CHAPTER EIGHTEEN

Two Hundred Dollar Doughnut

*O*ur son turned eighteen years old last week. We celebrated his birthday with his favorite steak and baked potato dinner followed by the cake he likes best—chocolate, made from a mix. I could find no wrapping paper anywhere in the house, so his sister wrapped his gifts—a cordless telephone, jeans, and two sweaters—in the colored Sunday funny papers and tied them up with red yarn bows.

Russell will graduate from high school this year. He has big plans for his life, plans that include work at a Christian youth camp this summer and college at an out-of-state university this fall. Like generations of parents before me, as the end of May approaches, I find myself musing, "Where has the time gone?"

His dad and I wonder, ask each other weekly, "Have we taught Russell everything he needs to know? Have we forgotten anything?"

We know we have.

Randy and I believe we've done a fairly good job. Russell is a great kid who makes us proud to be his parents. But we also realize we haven't always done the *best* we could do. We've sometimes been lazy, have often behaved inconsistently, and have alternately made mountains out of molehills and molehills out of mountains.

We have messed up with discouraging regularity.

We are sure of it.

And that makes us nervous, especially as the day that he will leave us draws closer and closer.

Last week, Randy and I became concerned about certain worrisome aspects of Russell's behavior. Both of us had recently noticed in our son a less than enthusiastic work ethic, a slacking up on family responsibilities, and poor handling of his monthly allowance. Minor issues perhaps, but issues that we believe relate to his maturity and his readiness to be on his own. So, in response to the problems (and mindful every minute that we don't have much time left), we sat him down to engage in the most dreaded of all family events—the Very Serious Talk.

The conversation began well, I thought. Randy and I talked to Russell about how he would be on his own very soon, and we explained that there were some matters we needed to discuss with him. He perked up at the words *on your own* and seemed to be listening with respectful attention.

At least he did until we got to the nitty-gritty part of the Very Serious Talk. Randy explained to Russell we could see that lately, he was Not Taking Care Of Business, Being Lazy About Chores, and Wasting Money.

Russell did not agree. He countered that he Was Too, Was Not, and Was Not, in a *slightly* defensive tone, I might add.

You could say that the Very Serious Talk took a turn south after that. In a rush of words fueled by impending separation anxiety, Randy and I lectured and corrected and nagged. Not at the same time of course. We politely took turns. Several turns each, in fact.

Our Russell is a smart boy. He knows when he's out-numbered—when it is best not to say *anything*. So after his initial outburst, he just sat on his hands and nodded deep understanding. The addition of Russell's well-spaced "yes ma'ams" and "no sirs" let us know that he was awake and provided just enough fuel to keep our verbal fires going.

Once we got warmed up, neither Randy or I could find a place to stop. I've had the same feeling driving seventy miles an hour down an interstate, *wanting* to get off, needing to go to the bathroom or wanting to get some lunch, but missing one exit after another. By the time we *finally* did run out of words (I think it was Randy who just ran out of air in mid-sentence), Russell was ready to Take Care of Business, Be Responsible, and Manage His Money Better.

Forever.

Scout's honor.

And could he please go to bed now?

Our children attend a small, rural, public school. And while they may miss out on *some* educational opportunities that would be available on a larger campus, Randy and I believe they gain a great deal from the setting we've chosen for them. Class sizes are generally smaller, our children's teachers are also our friends, and the administration's style of operating is, for the most part, in keeping with the small-town values Randy and I hold dear.

Students who attend small schools, because of less competition, enjoy the opportunity to participate in a wide variety of extra-curricular activities. Russell participates in athletics, choir, drama, academic competitions, and student council. These activities take up lots of time. He attends football practice after school, play practice in the evening, and studies for a current events' competitions at night on his own.

Russell especially enjoys his participation in student council. The club meets monthly, performs community service, and takes a yearly trip to the state convention.

To raise money for their various activities, the members of the student council hold several fundraisers. They wash cars, hold bake sales, and every year cook and serve a delicious homecoming spaghetti supper. And, every Friday, before time for class to start, members of the group also set up a card table and sell doughnuts to their fellow students.

Now Russell is not too crazy about washing cars and cooking spaghetti, but he *loves* to sell doughnuts. Assigned to the elementary campus, every Friday he looks forward to taking orders from his "regular" customers. Russell knows them by both their names and their doughnut preferences: plain, glazed, or chocolate frosted, one doughnut or two.

Janice is six years old. Missing her front teeth and yet *still* able to whistle, she always requests "a clear one, please." Russell takes her 35 cents. He knows she wants glazed.

Pedro speaks little English. He likes chocolate. Every week, his daddy gives him a quarter, probably unaware that doughnuts cost 35 cents. And every week, while Pedro waits patiently, Russell, when no one is looking, digs in his pocket for a dime to make up the difference.

The kindergartners and first graders, Russell's favorites, have little understanding of dollars and cents, so he has become deft at explaining over and over to the students that they can purchase *two* doughnuts for a dollar and still get some change back. The children who bring dollars make their sticky purchases and skip away, smug in the belief they've gotten a really great deal. *Everyone* knows that the kind of money that makes noise is *much* better than the kind of money you have to fold.

Last Friday, skinned-kneed, pony-tailed Marcie stood third in line to buy her doughnut. Russell waited patiently while she debated between plain and chocolate.

"I want chocolate," Marcie decided after great consideration.

"One or two?" Russell asked.

"One."

Russell waited while Marcie opened her pink plastic purse and located her money.

"Is this enough?" she asked hopefully.

Russell took two bills from Marcie, gave one back to her and reached into the money bag for the 65 cents she was due in change. "You have plenty of money. Wait a minute and I'll give you some change."

Then Russell the doughnut man took another look at the paper money Marcie had handed him. It was a *one hundred dollar bill.*

"Uh . . . uh . . . wait just a minute. Uh . . . Mrs. Johnson," he called for the student council sponsor. "Could you come here for a minute? I've got . . . uh . . . Marcie's got. . . uh. . . I think we sorta have a little problem."

Turns out Marcie had not one, not two, but *twelve* one hundred dollar bills in her pink plastic purse.

❧ ❧

I would imagine that Marcie's parents, once they recover from the realization that their daughter took Daddy's *whole* cashed paycheck to school with her, will sit her down and sternly deliver one of those Very Serious Talks we parents are famous for.

While the two of them think of what to say, I have one piece of important advice to give: Get with it! Trust me. The end of May will be here before you know it.

Be happy, young man, while you are young, and let your heart give you joy in the days of your youth.
ECCLESIASTES 11:9

PART THREE

❧ ❧

In a Day's Work

CHAPTER NINETEEN

Of Love and Lice

She wore blue jean shorts and a ruffled red dress that was supposed to button up the back. Except it had no buttons. Her feet were barefoot and though she *was* wearing underwear, one could assume it had not been changed in many, many days—for she reeked.

Bianca was only six years old, but motherless and unsupervised, she spent her days boldly roaming and scavenging the neighborhood. She *did* have a daddy, but his afternoons and nights were spent toiling at an all-night restaurant job. Mornings, the weary, sore-footed man slept on a sheet under various shade trees in his back yard, migrating almost hourly from one spot to another, searching for a little shade, groping for a place that was at all cooler than the inside of his oven-like, cinder block-constructed house.

His little girl, Bianca, received little attention.

Busy neighborhood mamas complained to each other about Bianca's pilfering of their own well-behaved children's toys. They gossiped about how she ran the streets half naked and how she urinated in the alley. They talked about how with no shame, the demanding little girl—surprisingly sturdily built, even a bit chubby—routinely appeared in their doorways at mealtimes. Eager to get on with their own dinners, the mamas most often shoved a tortilla, sometimes with a few beans wrapped inside, toward her and urged her to go home to her own house.

But Bianca paid no heed to their impatient shooings. Instead of skipping home, she plopped right down on their front stoops and stayed there until she finished their generous, though begrudged, meals. Only when the last crumb of food was gone would she scamper off, and then not toward home, but to another mama's house to extort more food if she was still hungry, or if she was thirsty, a cup of water.

As medical mission campaigns go, this trip had been an unusually trying one for the whole team. During the week, we workers expect to travel to two, three, or even four different locations to set up our free mobile clinics. Hours and hours spent together in van-imposed fellowship is normal, and generally we find the lengthy travel schedule not terribly difficult. We use the mechanically hypnotic down-time to sleep, read, talk, or reflect. But twice this week, treks we expected to complete in three hours ended up, because of unexpected, hair-pin-turning, heart-pounding mountain range roads, eating up almost eight hours of scheduled work time.

By mid-week, one of our team members was experiencing painfully swollen feet and hands. We were all concerned about her and I felt sure the heat was mostly to blame. The Mexican climate in this area close to the equator was more intense than anything even we hot-blooded Texans had experienced. Without the luxury of air conditioning or even electric fans, this week had been so sweltering we had joked about having to mop sweat from our brows even while we stood under cold showers.

Because of repeated heavy turnouts of very sick patients early in the week, our packed-into-boxes makeshift pharmacy was running short on some of our most-used medicines. This drug shortage would make the last day of the campaign frustrating. We would be forced to hand hurting and hopeful folks a paper prescription instead of the actual medicine they needed. Most of them would not have the money to have the written prescriptions filled.

And the van was making worrisome noises. Loud ones.

So it was that we arrived at the week's final clinic site hot, road-weary, swollen, and tired. And though not one of us spoke it, I think the entire team was ready to finish up and get home.

After exchanging handshakes and hugs with the minister of the church where we would hold the afternoon clinic, we appreciatively sipped the warm Cokes his wife brought us. Once we'd stretched our legs a bit we began to unload supplies and prepare for the patients who were already gathering in the church yard. Utilizing easily moved church pews, we efficiently sectioned off examination areas for the two physicians, a dental treatment area, a pharmacy section, and a corner where the children could gather for Bible stories and crafts while their parents waited for treatment. Each team member had a job.

Neil, James, Randy, Lewis, and Matt would treat livestock, mostly by deworming them. They gathered their equipment—ropes, tongs, medicine, and administration devices—loaded them into the bed of a local cowboy's pickup, and hopped in, ready to be taken to the outskirts of town where most of the town's animals were kept.

Stacy claimed a well-lit spot by the window and set up the dental chair (actually a reclining lawn chair wedged snugly into an elevated wooden platform built especially to hold it). She methodically laid out dental instruments, gloves, gauze, and sterilizing solutions.

Deborah, in the children's corner, prepared quickly. No doubt she would, as always, be the first member of the team to become really busy. Children seemed drawn to her and the minute the clinic opened, she would be surrounded by them. So for the fifth time this week, Deborah unpacked carefully chosen Bible story books and arranged within easy reach scissors, glue, stickers and glitter, coffee cans of crayons, and stacks of coloring book pictures of Jesus. She would be ready.

Shirley, Rachel, Angela, and I set up the pharmacy. We unpacked and arranged the medicines in alphabetical order on pews we moved together to form a U-shape. Stock bottles of vitamins, acetaminophen, and ibuprofen were divided into smaller, individual containers and carefully labeled.

Finally, we were ready for patients.

We were not, however, ready for Bianca.

While other children clutched their fathers' hands and clung to their mothers' skirts, Bianca marched into the church like she owned the place. She crawled under the pews to get inside the pharmacy area, swished her hands in the dentist's sterilizing solution, and claimed all the red crayons for herself. She toppled stacks of medicine, pawed through the doctors' bags, and mocked Deborah's earnest attempts to sing "Jesus Loves Me" in Spanish.

And she scratched her head. Constantly. It was obvious to tell, without even getting too close, that Bianca's long hair, dirty and matted, was heavily infested with lice.

We tried to be nice to the little girl without getting too close, to redirect her behavior, to correct her rowdiness, and finally, to gently get rid of her! In a day and a half, we would be home with our families. We were not unkind to the child, but none of us were eager to take crawling insect tag-a-longs back to Texas with us. It just wasn't worth it.

At least that's how *I* felt.

The afternoon wore on. As always, we treated lots of sick folks, dispensed lots of medicine, did a lot of good.

It was as we were preparing to pack up, wash, and eat dinner that I first missed Angela. I realized I hadn't seen her in more than an hour. Glancing around, I still couldn't find her. Other team members began to look for her. We searched outside, in the bathroom, in the van—but found no Angela. Finally, when I poked my head into an unused Sunday School classroom, I saw her.

I motioned to the other searchers. The room was dimly lit, but we could see Angela, near a window, sitting quietly in a rickety folding chair cradling Bianca in her arms. The little girl was snuggled close, with her head on Angela's chest, her lanky arms and legs curled tightly into the fetal position. As Angela slowly rocked back and forth in the chair, Bianca, transformed from a street-wise little pest into the needy baby she was, sucked her thumb and absently rubbed her sticky fingers through Angela's long blond hair. A far away expression graced the child's face and I hoped, needed to believe, she was remembering a mother who, at one time, held her close.

No one spoke. I'm not sure anyone even *breathed*.

Finally Angela looked up and saw her doorway audience. Her grin and her shrug broke the scene's spell and she spoke, "So what if you get lice? You can always get rid of them."

Not so tired anymore, no longer quite so eager to pack up and head home, we relaxed and smiled back at her.

And one by one, we admired Bianca's pretty dress.

Gave her a cookie.

Tickled her toes.

Kissed her dirty little face.

Wiped away our own repentant tears.

And remembered why we had come.

And whoever welcomes a little child like this
in my name welcomes me.
Matthew 18:5

CHAPTER TWENTY

High School and Headbands

When my daughter was a baby, she loved to totter around in my high heels and drape herself with colored beads and gold and silver-colored chains pillaged from my jewelry box. She couldn't wait to have her ears pierced just like me, and she begged to wear our matching mother-daughter dresses every Sunday. In her eyes, Miss America's beauty and intelligence paled in comparison to mine, even if I couldn't twirl a baton.

But in a scenario my friends already living with adolescent girls tried to warn me of, one that reminds me of the tale of Sleeping Beauty, my steep ranking plummeted overnight. Shortly after her twelfth birthday, Rachel went to sleep a gawky little girl and woke up the next morning a curvy, graceful young woman with high cheekbones, silky long eyelashes, and her own ideas about beauty.

Now approaching her thirteenth birthday, she is thrilled to be growing up. Though I know her increasing needs for privacy and independence are normal and healthy, I admit adjusting to this hormone-fueled phase of my daughter's life has been difficult for me.

Shopping for clothes is not much fun. When I point out items I think are pretty and appropriate, Rachel rolls her eyes or, even worse, giggles. Defensively, I point out other mall shoppers and how nice they looked in similar outfits.

Possessing her own sense of style, Rachel groans, "Mom, some women have *no* taste."

With much effort, I am learning not to get my feelings hurt when my haircut is deemed out-of-style and my clothing old-fashioned, sometimes even embarrassing. I'm told this is normal, and as long as Rachel doesn't behave disrespectfully, I'm usually able to tolerate her critical assessments of my appearance. Though doing so is not easy for me, I try to remember that her actions are normal adolescent assertions of independence.

So, considering my case of overnight fashion ignorance, I was surprised when Rachel asked if she could borrow a headband. Scavenging in my top dresser drawer for socks (the only items in my wardrobe she still covets) Rachel unearthed a handmade fabric-and-leather band I've owned for several years.

"Where did you get this? Why haven't you ever worn it, Mom?"

My husband is a coach. The life we've chosen is a good one, and I am enriched by the relationships and friendships I've forged with other coaches' wives. When getting settled in a new town, I quickly become acquainted with the wives of my husband's co-workers. Camaraderie comes naturally. I enjoy sharing with women who understand the long hours my husband works, the criticism he sometimes faces from the community, the letdowns he experiences when his team is losing. Knowing a built-in support group awaits me has made moving from one community to another easier.

Only once, several years ago, did I find this to be untrue. Though I don't believe the snubs were intentional, I felt them just the same. I simply couldn't find my niche in the group of coaches' wives in our new town. There had been little turnover in the athletic staff in recent years, so perhaps the wives were already so close to each other they didn't recognize my friendly overtures.

When I climbed the bleachers to the section reserved for the families of coaches to watch a game, there never seemed to be a place for me to sit. When I attempted to start conversations with these woman, my words fell flat. Repeatedly I initiated get-togethers for all the coach's wives, but the dates I chose were usually inconvenient for most of them.

After months spent trying and failing at making friends with them, after enduring many of the unpleasant feelings I thought I'd left behind—those feelings of being uncomfortable and excluded by the high school "in" crowd—I simply gave up and developed other relationships. I soon had plenty to keep me busy with church and work and children and my home. And I became content in our new home.

There were only a few times a year that I *had* to socialize with the wives' group. One of those occasions was the annual Coaches' Christmas Party. We had lived in the community for several years by then and had dared not miss one of these basically mandatory end-of-year events. In the beginning, I had wondered, *how bad can a Christmas party be?*

I was right to wonder. Despite my best intentions, somehow, at each party, I managed to do something wrong. At the first get-together, having been told the gathering would be "casual," I wore jeans and an embroidered holiday sweatshirt.

I arrived to find the other wives decked out in velvet jumpers and velour pantsuits.

The next year I wore a red and green plaid skirt and a new silk blouse. My friend Sheri is the epitome of good taste.

Sympathetic to my fashion faux pas the year before, she expertly helped me put the outfit together and assured me I looked gorgeous.

I was the only woman at the party not wearing jeans and sneakers. Not only was I overdressed, at *that* party I managed to spill red punch on the hostess' new white carpet.

Another year, Randy forgot to tell me I was assigned to furnish a sliced ham for the buffet. I understood why my mandarin orange fruit salad was not happily received by the chairman of the food committee. She had carefully planned her menu around the contribution she had expected me to bring.

But the very last party we attended there is the one I can't forget.

As was tradition, we each brought a wrapped gift to exchange. Men and women's gifts were separated, the packages were numbered, and each person drew from a hat a slip of paper indicating the order in which he or she would choose a gift. The rule was that if you did not like the present you unwrapped, you could take someone else's already opened gift and give them yours. They, in turn, could force a trade with someone else.

A spending limit of only ten dollars was set, but everyone went to great lengths to find unusual, attractive, or useful items. Socks, flashlights, and fancy screwdrivers were popular with the coaches, while the wives favored scented candles, Christmas ornaments, and costume jewelry. Every year, there were at least two or three gifts that became the hit of the night. Every guest at the party would hope to keep a coveted item, only to have it repeatedly "stolen" from them by a person whose number came after theirs.

This year, I was going to get *one* thing right. My gift would be the object of desire of every woman there. I had purchased it while on a trip to Guatemala, and it was truly lovely. I wrapped the handmade, multicolored, beautifully crafted headband in tissue paper and splurged on a fancy gift bag.

We arrived at the party on time, and I was thrilled to be dressed correctly. My husband's boss raved about the bacon cheese rolls I'd brought, and I managed to drink all my punch without spilling a drop. I was actually enjoying the party.

It was only during the gift exchange that things began to go wrong. *How could I have made such a mistake?* My gift, un-wrapped by guest number two, was not the most coveted gift, as I'd just *known* it would be, but the most maligned. No one liked it. They laughed at it and wondered aloud who had brought it.

It was like being trapped in a Junior High nightmare. I said nothing, but felt my face grow hot and I began to squirm. Woman after woman received it in trade, and promptly traded it to someone else. I was reminded of the childhood game "hot potato." It seemed the focus of the night's enter-tainment was to see who would end up with the ridiculous gift. Finally, mercifully, it was my turn, and I took the gift for my own and prayed the evening would end quickly.

That dreadful, ridiculous night occurred almost ten years ago. The whole situation seems silly now, but even after all this time, I can't seem to bring myself to wear what I still con-sider to be a beautiful accessory.

❦

"Mom, this is a cool headband."

"You think so?"

"Oh yeah. It's really pretty. Could I wear it sometime?"

"Sure, sweetie. Today if you like."

"Thanks, Mom."

This morning I stood in the hall and watched my beauti-ful woman-child Rachel bounce out the door crowned with *my* headband. I smiled when I remembered the party where the object of her fashionable desire was scorned by my peers.

And I muse that Rachel and I disagree about almost everything these days. But on one matter we are of exactly the same mind. *Some women just have no taste.*

Like mother, like daughter.
Ezekiel 16:44

CHAPTER TWENTY-ONE

Land of Flying Fish

*J*uan was dressed for the weather in shorts and a T-shirt. He wore his shoes in the style universally favored by five-year-olds—on the wrong feet. His mama *had* scrubbed his face and combed his hair this morning, but that was hours ago and little evidence remained of her motherly ministrations. An obedient little boy, he sat right where his mama told him to, on a wooden bench between bossy cousin Pedro and baby sister Maria.

Senorita Rosa was telling the children a story. She was pretty and smelled like flowers. The cookies she gave everyone tasted yummy. Maybe there would be more cookies later. Coloring the picture of Jesus and the children had been fun, but why did mean old Pedro get the purple crayon, the best one in the whole box?

Juan sat quietly and listened to Senorita Rosa tell a Bible story. Or at least he tried to.

It is sometimes hard to sit still. Really hard.

First Juan's legs began to swing.

Just a little bit, and *very* slowly.

Then a bit faster.

Soon, almost by themselves, his arms began to move and his head began to bob.

Finally, totally lost in play, he began to sway and hum, softly at first, then louder.

"Jesus is your friend. You can talk to him any time you want to," Senorita Rosa continued telling the children.

"Zoom," went the toy in Juan's hands. "Zoom . . . Zoom . . . ZOOM!" Before he knew it, the toy the lady's friend had given him—not even an airplane, but a pink plastic fish—was flying back and forth over and around and above the distracted heads of the fourteen loosely organized but, up until now, intently interested Bible students.

Suddenly Pedro began to laugh and point at Juan. "Juan thinks fish can fly. Ha ha ha!" he tormented.

That no-good Pedro. Just because he is ten years old he thinks he can pick on anybody he wants.

Bible story now forgotten, the other children joined in. "Fish can't fly!"

"Juan is stupid!"

"Juan is crazy!"

"Everybody knows only birds can fly! Not fish! Ha ha ha!"

Senorita Rosa clapped her hands and hushed them.

Stung by his peers and now afraid of his pretty teacher, Juan hung his head. He was in big trouble. The plastic fish, now scorned, lay in the dirt at his feet.

Senorita Rosa spoke to the children. "What do you mean fish can't fly. Of course they can! Close your eyes. Every one of you," she ordered them. "Close them tightly. Now, what can you see?"

"Nuh-thing," the children answered in unison.

It was true. With their eyes closed, they were oblivious to the scrap wood shacks bordering the alley-turned-classroom in which they sat. They could no longer see the twice-picked-over garbage strewn in the street below them, the sheets of rusted tin surrounding the muddy yard, the exhausted faces of their parents who waited in line to receive free medical care our team had come to give them.

"*My* fish can fly," Senorita Rosa told them dreamily.

I looked up from the open-air, makeshift pharmacy in which I was working and listened intently to her words. I marveled at the contrast between the young woman's exquisite beauty—she reminded me of a Mexican Barbie doll—and the ugly urban squalor around her.

She was in control of the children. "When I close my eyes, my fish can jump and fly and sing and dance. My fish is beautiful and he can even talk. What can your fish do?"

The wriggly children were hers. Totally.

"Mine can run!"

"Wonderful!"

"Mine can ride a bike!"

"Really!"

"Mine can eat bananas!"

"Oh my!" exclaimed their teacher.

"Now open your eyes and listen to what I'm going to tell you. It is very important and I never want you to forget it." The children leaned forward and listened intently, even the formerly spiteful Pedro, and especially the now beaming Juan.

"When you close your eyes anything is possible. When you stop and imagine—and you can do it any time you want to—fish can fly, trees can dance, oceans can sing. In your dreams you can see anything you want to see, go anywhere you want to go, be anyone you want to be. No matter what happens to you, never forget."

❧ ❧

People often ask *just why do I go to Mexico? Exactly what do we do on these short-term medical campaigns?* I explain that we check blood pressures and temperatures and we organize the pharmacy. Team members soothe crying babies and tired old ladies and remind arthritic patients to take their ibuprofen with food. We hurriedly unload supplies in the mornings and wearily load them back again in the evenings.

And in spite of our best efforts, we don't even make a dent in the sufferings of the people we come to serve. At the end of the week, we return to our homes sadly mindful of how much work we have left undone.

Then why, I'm often asked, *do you go?*

If I think the person *really* wants to know, if I know them well, I smile and request that they close their eyes for just a moment. They look at me curiously but usually comply.

Then while their eyes are closed, I ask them to imagine a beautiful tropical fish. *"Can you see the fish?"* I ask. *"Can you see the colors, the fins, the tail of the fish?"*

"Well, yes." They are a bit sheepish.

Then I tell them that I work in Mexico because a lovely sister in Christ, a woman named Rosa, taught me a lesson. She taught me to believe that fish really *can* fly.

With God all things are possible.
MATTHEW 19:26

CHAPTER TWENTY-TWO

Tender Is the Night

I've always loved bedtime. I enjoy the gentle ritual of locking the doors, turning off the lights, slipping between cool sheets, and hearing the final words my family speaks before sleep:

"Good night."

"See you in the morning."

"Sleep well."

"I love you."

"I love you too."

Because of her diminutive size, I would have guessed Jeri to be about twelve years old. Five feet tall and barely ninety pounds, her body, decked out in pink shorts and a Tweety bird T-shirt, looked more like that of a young boy than a developing adolescent girl—even one with a pretty face.

And Jeri *was* pretty. Her pixie-like face, graced with soft gray eyes and a turned up nose, was marred only by a thin, inch-long scar above her left eyebrow. The scar caught my eye and I found myself absently wondering how she'd gotten it. I smiled at her and commented on the creative way she'd styled her hair. Straight and straw-colored, she had pulled it up into a dozen elaborate African-American style braids. Each tiny skein of hair had been carefully secured with a different color rubber band.

From her counselor, I learned Jeri was not twelve, but almost seventeen years old. She lived with two teenage tent-mates, among thirty other campers at the therapeutic wilderness camp where I am employed as camp nurse.

Set deep in the forest, the facility accepts and attempts to help kids with wide varieties of problems. Teens ages 13 to 17 are placed at the camp for anywhere from six months to one year. They sleep in rustic shelters which they build themselves, do much of their own campfire cooking, and function without electricity or hot water at campsite. Though guided by compassionate, well-trained counselors, day-to-day the teens must rely heavily on each other to ensure their needs are met. The phrase printed on the business cards of my supervisor, the program's director, sums up the camp's goal: *Breaks the cycle of violence and failure . . . for their sake and ours.*

Jeri's counselor had brought her to my office so I could check an itchy rash she had on her left foot. Before assessing Jeri for what experience told me, without even looking, was most likely athlete's foot fungus, I admired her unusual ankle bracelet—an adornment she'd crafted of knotted-together ivory-colored beads and sand-smoothed seashells. I told her that I too, loved shells. Impulsively, she pulled the bracelet off and handed it to me. "You can have it. I'll make me another one."

I protested only a moment, then accepted the generous gift and proceeded to examine her foot. My guess was right. Jeri did have a severe case of athlete's foot. Not a big problem. The rash would easily be cleared up with clean socks and a twice-daily application of over-the-counter anti-fungal cream. But some precautions were in order: Other campers, I stressed to her, should carefully avoid direct contact with her inflamed foot. They should not share socks or shoes.

Hopefully, the fungus would not spread. Jeri understood. I thanked her again for the neat bracelet and told her I would recheck her in a week.

Later, at my desk, I poured a mug of coffee and settled in to read her file. All of the camp's young residents were placed at the facility because of behavioral problems—some serious and some not-so serious. Jeri's calm demeanor led me to believe she was likely one of the facility's less-troubled kids.

But sadly, my premature assessment of Jeri proved wrong. Prominent in her file were lengthy accounts of shoplifting, public intoxication, and even burglary. She had routinely skipped school since she was eleven years old and had already failed two grades. Last year she had assaulted her teacher and this year, just prior to her placement at camp, she had been suspended because of aggressive, increasingly violent behavior.

My coffee forgotten, I read further, and began to scan the file's section titled "Family History." First her birth . . . then age six months . . . one year . . . two . . . three . . . . The more I read, the sicker and more angry I felt inside. Child abuse is such a common factor in the lives of the teens living at the camp that, regrettably, I've stopped being surprised when I learn about it. But this account, this particular case, was much, much more extensive than anything I'd read before. Prior to her adoption at age five, the child Jeri, the tiny young woman whose foot I'd just held in my hand, had endured incident after incident of the most horrific abuse I have ever heard of. If I were to chronicle the five worst tragedies that I could think of—the five most horrible things that could be done to or happen to a child—they would have all occurred to Jeri before she was four years old.

I pictured Jeri as a young child, thought about what atrocities she had been subjected to, and became convinced that the fact that she was still alive, that her body and at least *some* of her soul were still intact, was a miracle. In spite of her acting out, her rebellion, her inexcusable behavior, she had survived.

I was thankful.

Jeri skipped into my office a week later, grinned when she noticed I was wearing the ankle bracelet she had given me and told me her rash had disappeared. The cream had worked. Since the rash was gone, she questioned, was it okay for tent-mate Shawn to go back to giving her foot rubs?

"Foot rubs? Shawn gives you foot rubs? When?" I questioned curiously. I had never seen Shawn, a pale and pudgy, rather withdrawn kind of kid, willingly interact or communicate with anyone except her caseworker.

"Every night. To help me go to sleep."

I learned that for as long as she could remember, Jeri had experienced great difficulty falling asleep. She would toss and turn and flail about in her bed. Her nervous insomnia only worsened when she came to camp and her sleeplessness distressed her tent-mates, Shawn and Mary. So to help Jeri go to sleep, every night Shawn positioned her metal cot so that its head was at the foot of Jeri's. She propped herself up on her elbows so that she could reach her friend's feet without getting out of her own bed. Sometimes she would use lotion and rub them hard, other times she would use her dry hands and stroke them very lightly.

"And that makes you fall asleep," I stated.

"Most of the time. It also helps when Mary reads the Bible to us," she answered.

"Mary," I repeated in disbelief, "reads the Bible. Out loud?" Surely I had misunderstood. Mary was the loudest, bossiest, most disruptive kid in the camp. Her uncontrolled emotions and fiery temper kept her in constant trouble. Mary was never "hot," she was "burning up." She wasn't cold, she was "freezing to death." Mary wasn't hungry, she was "starving," not tired, but "dying of exhaustion." One thing was for sure, with little regard for the needs or feelings of anyone else, Mary could always be found at the center of attention.

Jeri interrupted my thoughts. "Yep, she reads to me and Shawn at night. Her grandmother, before she died, told her to read a chapter in the Bible every single night before she goes to sleep. So she does. With her flashlight. At first she tried to make me and Shawn read too, but Shawn's not a very good reader and I don't have a Bible. So Mary reads out loud to us."

"Let me be sure I understand." My voice softened as I realized that in the midst of foot fungus and a shell bracelet I'd stumbled onto a scene as profoundly healing and holy as anything I'd ever experienced in church. "Every night you lie down on your cot. Shawn massages your feet. Mary reads the Bible."

"Yeah," she shrugged. "But I do stuff for them too. We take care of each other."

🙢 🙠

Tonight, lying quietly in my bed with my husband beside me, after I've checked all the doors and turned out the lights, I'll stare up at the ceiling. As I review my day, I'll picture in my mind an army-green tent pitched deep in the forest. I'll smell the scent of pine trees and I'll almost hear the sounds the crickets make. I'll imagine I feel a wind that blows from the north.

Transported, I'll hear rhythmic breathing, gentle sighs, and soft snoring. I'll think of Jeri and Shawn and Mary.

"Sleep well," I'll whisper to the darkness. "Sleep well."

Their eyes were heavy.
Mark 14:40

CHAPTER TWENTY-THREE

All Creatures Great and Small

My friend Jean works for a veterinarian. For the *young* Dr. Henry, son of the now retired *old* Dr. Henry. She's mostly assigned to the office so she answers the phones, makes appointments, and keeps the books. But the clinic where Jean is employed is a small one and sometimes she's called to the back to assist the doctor in examining and treating small animals brought in for his care. She enjoys the change of pace.

Jean has worked in the clinic for so long that by now, she knows a great deal about animals. Friends and neighbors often come to her for advice. If it happens to be after regular office hours and Dr. Henry is unreachable, folks have been known to call Jean at home to ask her their pet-related questions. She is patient with concerned animal owners and if she is able, she is happy to answer their queries.

Jean truly loves animals. Always has. Each evening when she arrives home, she is welcomed by a motley assortment of critters of her own.

First she's met by Albert, an affectionate, elderly, and overweight Greyhound dog. Albert always greets Jean at the end of her winding driveway and races her back to the house. Albert hates to lose so Jean often lets him win. He rewards her car's embarrassing lack of speed with a wide-mouthed, tooth-baring grin and a tail that wags so wildly it nearly knocks her down.

Next, from her hiding spot behind the rose bushes, Callie the cat appears. Callie is a long-haired calico and she loves to hunt. About twice a week, Jean comes home to find, left on her doorstep, the sad remains of some slow moving rodent, a sacrificial victim of Callie's cunning skill. If Jean neglects to feign pleasure at Callie's proud and generous front stoop offering, the cat is likely to trail right off in a snooty feline snit. She might not even show up until suppertime.

Once Jean has gone into the house and put the kettle on for a pot of tea, she'll pull on rubber boots and a jacket and trek to the barn to feed horse Lucy. Usually Lucy will be standing near the gate, worrying the feed trough, anxious for her dinner. But if she's not, Jean will know right where to find her. She'll look out across the pasture and, sure enough, Lucy will be standing inside an open-ended horse trailer.

Waiting.

To go.

For while many horses abhor trailers and traveling and go almost crazy with anxiety when forced near a wheeled contraption of any kind, Lucy loves both. Several times a week, hopeful that some kind soul will exit the highway and come and take her for a ride—somewhere, anywhere—Lucy will go and wait in the trailer. Sometimes she'll stand there patiently for half a day or more.

And occasionally, Jean will chuckle, break down, hitch up the trailer, and take Lucy for a ride.

Jean doesn't just love animals, she also cares for their sometimes distraught owners she knows from the clinic. She understands the pain of a new widow who is forced to put her late husband's faithful but arthritic old hound to sleep. Jean knows how scary it is to watch a mother cat give birth for the first time and she is gentle when she explains to the cat's owner that she is sorry, but *no, the vet does not make house calls to deliver kittens.* Jean is patient when she explains, once again, which vaccinations and tests are necessary, which are optional, and what are the best foods to feed puppies, parakeets, pigmy goats, and pot-bellied pigs.

Jean has a special soft spot in her heart for elderly pet owners. So does Dr. Henry. And though they don't exactly advertise the fact, their older clients are allowed to charge their pet's fees and pay them out monthly.

Ada, in her eighties, shares her apartment with an equally geriatric poodle. Little Fifi, in her old age, has started coming down with increasingly frequent infections and has developed the unfortunate ability to digest only the pricey dog food sold at the clinic.

Tom, only fifty years old but confined to a wheelchair, owns a black Labrador Retriever that recently required complicated surgery to relieve debilitating hip pain. The lab is his constant companion and Tom would have been lost without the dog.

A.J., ninety-two years old, owns a black cat named Midnight. The wiry little cat, though neutered years ago, still picks frequent fights with felines twice his size and has required emergency treatment twice in the last three months. Expensive, after-hours treatment.

And then there is Mrs. Goolsby. On a fixed income, the elderly and sometimes eccentric woman takes in stray after stray. So many hurt, hungry, and homeless animals of all kinds show up at her back door one is led to believe that the woman must have a sign in her yard (visible only by critters of the four-footed variety), proclaiming *Kind Woman, Free Food.*

Mrs. Goolsby buys cat and dog food by the case, and almost weekly she brings sick, wounded, and as far as anyone knows, unvaccinated animals to the clinic. Jean helps Mrs. Goolsby find homes for many of the animals and the veterinarian gives her the Senior Citizen discount, but even so, the woman's bill sometimes threatens to reach four digits.

Mrs. Goolsby, on a fixed income, will never pay it off.

And so it was no surprise when on a Friday afternoon, just before closing time, Mrs. Goolsby once again came hurrying into the vet clinic, bearing a trembling but silent, wounded, bath towel-wrapped *something* in her arms.

"What have you got with you today, Mrs. Goolsby? A cat or a dog?" Jean asked as she pulled the woman's file.

"Neither," she answered. "It's a chicken this time. A hen I think."

"A chicken?" Had she heard right?

"Yes."

"Did she come up in your yard?"

"Oh no," Mrs. Goolsby answered. "She fell off a truck, a Pilgrim's Pride chicken truck. You know those big trucks with just cages and cages of chickens stacked up on them?" Mrs. Goolsby's hands fluttered in front of her. "She fell off one of those."

Jean knew of which trucks Mrs. Goolsby spoke. The vehicle she described was one used to haul the chickens to processing plants. Any chicken who rode one of *those* trucks was destined not for the farm or the range, but for the skillet or the roasting pan, for a salad or a fricassee. This chicken was about to be made into dinner.

"Anyway, I was driving home from the beauty shop and I saw this pretty white chicken fall off the truck and roll into the ditch. So I pulled over and picked her up. I think she's got a broken leg. Is Dr. Henry still here?"

"Yes ma'am. He's still here. Just have a seat."

Jean popped her head into an exam room, broke the news to Dr. Henry. "Mrs. Goolsby just came in."

"Dog or cat?"

"Neither," she answered. "Chicken. Hen, she thinks."

"A *hen*?" he repeated.

"Fell off a Pilgrim's Pride truck."

"Mrs. Goolsby?"

"No! The chicken."

He shook his head.

The news was not good. Dr. Henry stroked the trembling white hen. "Mrs. Goolsby," he spoke gently, "we can't save her. She has too many broken bones. No matter what I did for her, she just wouldn't ever be all right."

"You can't do anything for her? Are you sure?"

"Yes ma'am. I'm sure. We need to put her to sleep."

The woman's face clouded. "She's such a pretty little thing. I just hate it." She wiped her eyes. "But I don't want her to suffer. Do what you think best."

Jean saw her out.

❦ ❦

Mrs. Goolsby passed away herself several months ago. I often wonder how many animals she cared for in her lifetime, how many bowls of food and fresh water she poured out, how many vaccinations she paid for.

Some might think it silly to care so much for an animal— a dog or a cat or even a little white chicken. But I think there's a part of most of us, *a good part* of us, that understands and welcomes the compassion a helpless animal stirs in us.

And like Mrs. Goolsby, we do what we think best.

Give her the reward she has earned,
And let her works bring her praise at the city gate.
PROVERBS 31:31

CHAPTER TWENTY-FOUR

Fall from Grace

G race and I became best friends in the sixth grade. We shared sweatshirts and sneakers, secrets and cereal. Neither of us had a boyfriend, though many of our early-blooming classmates did. Since we had each other, our lack of male companionship didn't bother us much.

I was devastated when Grace and her family moved away in the spring of that year. Grace hated to leave too and so she and I vowed we'd stay best friends forever. And at first, we did—penning each other long detailed letters on lined kitten-and-rainbow-decorated stationary. But gradually and predictably, our letters became fewer and farther between until we finally lost touch with each other.

Fifteen years later, when I started my new job at a home health agency in the town where I grew up, I was thrilled to find that Grace, too, was employed there. Grace, like me, had entered nursing school right out of high school, and also like me, she had married her college sweetheart and was raising a family. We easily rekindled our girlhood friendship.

When she was my childhood companion, Grace had been silly, fond of practical jokes, and full of life. I was tickled to find that my funny friend, though all grown up now, still possessed a hilariously wicked wit. An animated storyteller, she kept the whole office doubled over in side-splitting stitches at the riotous tales she told of her madly disorganized household and the shameless shenanigans of her four rowdy boys. When Grace was around I laughed so much I found it practically impossible to finish my afternoon nurse's notes and had to constantly scurry around to catch up on my paperwork.

Grace, perpetually disorganized and late, every workday would storm into the office for her daily assignment, tying her sneakers with one hand and pulling her shiny black hair up in a scrunchy with the other. With that minimal effort, Grace managed to look better than the rest of us who'd spent a good bit of our mornings wrestling with blow dryers and hot rollers. Her sparkling blue eyes, framed by thick lashes, needed no mascara and her skin was so smooth she wore only a smudge of powder. Even dressed in the baggy scrub suits she favored for work, Grace's curvy size six figure was a source of intense torment for those of us who sipped our lunchtime Slim Fast while she feasted on jelly sandwiches and Little Debbie snack cakes.

Grace's regular patients loved her and asked for her by name. She cared for them with kindness and compassion. Her clinical techniques were top notch and her assessment skills were excellent. If I occasionally needed to take a day or two off work, I could leave my assigned patients in her care with the assurance they would be well cared for while I was gone. The home health agency was lucky to have her.

Two years after our friendship's renewal Grace resigned from her position, so I helped throw a big going-away party for her. Though all of us hated to see her leave, we understood and wished her well. Her husband, Sam, had been offered a new job and the family would be moving to another part of the state.

Once again, Grace and I promised to keep in touch, and once again, after a few months, our letters and calls to each other became less and less frequent. When she'd been gone almost three years, with guilt, I realized we'd not communicated in more than six months. That very afternoon I tried to phone her, but my call would not go through. So I sent her a card. It was returned to me weeks later with no forwarding address.

Several years passed and I almost forgot about Grace. After so much time, I did not expect to see her again. Like Grace, my own life's path had taken some unexpected turns. I'd had another baby, and we had moved to a new house. When Dr. Fitzpatrick, a young physician I admired and respected, announced his need for an office nurse, I changed jobs, leaving my home health agency position to work in his family practice clinic.

My employer's booming practice encompassed a broad scope of medical services to the community. As a result, my duties in his clinic were wide and varied. I performed lab tests, developed x-ray films, ran cardiograms, and prepared patients for procedures. I also assisted with Worker's Compensation examinations and pre-employment physicals. A big part of my day was spent fielding phone calls from folks who needed refills on medications or who had questions about their prescribed treatments or diets. Because the doctor's practice was so busy, I worked as efficiently as possible to keep him on schedule. He had a tendency to dawdle over patients, I thought, and sometimes I would become critical and resentful at having to stay late due to his lack of timely work habits.

So I was less than thrilled when at four-thirty one afternoon, I intercepted a call from the local jail about a prisoner who was complaining of chest pain. Could they bring the inmate in to see the doctor?

"How long has the pain been present?" I asked.

"Since about two," answered the jailer.

"Any shortness of breath?"

"No."

"Nausea?"

"No."

"Sweating?"

"No."

It doesn't sound like a heart attack, I tried to convince my-self, *probably gas or an upset stomach. Russell has soccer practice at five-thirty, I've got PTA at seven . . . I really need to get off on time today!*

"Are you *sure* it can't wait until tomorrow? We could make an appointment for first thing in the morning."

"No ma'am, I don't think so. The pain's pretty bad."

I knew better than to delay seeing a patient, and instinc-tively, my good nursing judgment won over my intense desire to go home. "Come to the back door," I instructed the officer. "I'll be watching for you and I'll have an exam room ready."

Since I'd just assumed the prisoner was male, I was sur-prised when, fifteen minutes later, I looked out and saw the jailer leading a young woman toward the clinic's rear en-trance. Head down, shoulders bent, plump and pale, she was dressed in a county-issue olive green sweat suit. She wore on her feet ill-fitting, gray plastic shower shoes.

Anxious to get her in—and hopefully out—as quickly as possible, I held the heavy door open for her. Just inside the clinic's entrance, the woman's heel slipped out of her shoe causing her to stumble and almost fall. Only when I reached out to steady her did she raise her head.

It was Grace.

Grace was no longer married to Sam and her life was no longer just like mine. She'd been divorced for two years, and her boys, now teenagers, lived with their father. Single for the first time in twenty years, things had been okay for awhile, she told me. But she became restless and was so very lonely that she decided to move back to her former hometown. Once there, she realized she no longer felt comfortable with her married friends. So she joined a new, younger group and began frequenting local nightclubs and bars. Less than a year ago, she had been arrested for the first time in her life—for drunk driving. She had gone to court, paid her fine, and been released. The whole incident had been humiliating and humbling and she had vowed that she would get her act together and it would never happen again.

But it did happen again. Twice. And because of this most recent arrest she would serve time in the county jail.

I had absolutely no idea what to say to Grace. I felt uncomfortable and embarrassed. The person sitting before me bore no resemblance in appearance or in character to the person I'd once called my best friend. I felt both appalled and repelled at what Grace had become.

Alone with her in the exam room, I tried to speak in a calm, professional, "nurse" voice, but my words felt stilted and awkward and my cheerfulness sounded fake even to my own ears. "Tell me about your chest pain. When did it start? Are you having it now? Does exertion make it worse?"

For though I could see great pain in Grace's eyes, I could find no signs of it in her body. Her blood pressure and pulse rate were normal and her breathing was even and unlabored.

"Annette, my chest is fine."

"Are you short of breath?"

"No."

"Arm or neck hurting?"

"No."

"Any nausea?"

"None."

"Then why . . . ?" I questioned.

"I lied to the jailers to get them to bring me here. I'm going to ask Dr. Fitzpatrick to put me in the hospital—just for tonight. I *have* to be put in the hospital."

"Grace, are you sick?" I tried again.

"No, I'm not sick. My oldest son joined the Marines and he's scheduled to leave for Saudi Arabia in four days—Desert Storm. I haven't seen him in eight months. I'm not allowed to have visitors until next Sunday, and the only way I can be with him before he leaves is if I'm a patient in the hospital."

I was silent, but fuming.

"Grace, I don't know if he can do that." I fidgeted with my stethoscope and avoided looking into her eyes. "He can't admit you if there is no medical reason."

What was she thinking? I wondered. *I can see she wants to see her son, but there are rules. She's a nurse. She should know he can't just admit anyone to the hospital. There has to be a valid diagnosis. What if he did and someone found out? She's placing him in a terrible position by even asking.*

After spending more than an hour in the exam room with her, Dr. Fitzpatrick made the necessary calls to have Grace admitted to the hospital. *She must have put on a really good act,* I thought.

Once she had left the clinic, I tidied up the exam room, then feigning ignorance, I asked Dr. Fitzpatrick about Grace. Was she seriously ill? What was her diagnosis?

"Heart trouble," he told me without blinking, "serious heart trouble. I've admitted her to the hospital for treatment."

❧ ❦

I was right that day. About the rules and all. Grace didn't deserve for a minute the favor she was asking of Dr. Fitzpatrick. She had done something wrong and she should have been willing to accept the consequences of her actions.

But on this day, I find myself on my knees offering up prayers for forgiveness of *my* wrongs. And as I do so, I can find no comfort in remembering my rightness that day. No comfort at all.

Judgment without mercy will be shown
to anyone who has not been merciful.
JAMES 2:13

CHAPTER TWENTY-FIVE

A Black Cat, a Cut Lip, and a Bad Case of Chicken Pox

randma and Mother blamed it on the black cat. Today marked the first day of school, the *very* first day of first grade, and Margaret was ready. Excited. She wore a new blue dress, new black shoes, and carried a brand new lunchbox. *And,* stashed in her book bag, were a new, lined, Big Chief tablet and two fat practice pencils. Margaret couldn't wait to get to school, had looked forward to this day all summer long. Today she had woken up and gotten herself completely dressed and ready so early that she had pestered her mother for more than an hour, had nearly worried her mother *to death* in fact, asking every five minutes if it was time to go *yet.*

And at last, it was. Once she'd set their breakfast dishes in the sink and run hot water over them, Mother tied on a head-scarf, applied lipstick, grabbed her purse, dug for her keys, and instructed Margaret to get in the car.

Margaret did not have to be told twice. Clutching her book bag, she jumped right into the front seat of the car and rolled down the window so she could see better. Mother put the car in gear and inched out of the driveway, onto the dirt road in front of the house, and started slowly toward the five-mile-away school house.

Suddenly and unexpectedly nervous, Margaret fiddled with the waistband of her new dress and picked at the cuticle on her right thumb. *What if she was late for school? What if they locked the door and didn't let you in if you didn't make it on time?*

Though Mother made a leisurely start, once down the road a piece, she turned on the radio, glanced at her watch, and sped up a bit. Margaret let out her breath, looked out the window, and thought that perhaps she *would* make it to school on time.

Or maybe she wouldn't. When they were still three miles from school, out of nowhere, a shiny black cat appeared on the right and sprinted across the road in front of the car. Mother slammed on the brakes and at the same time, reflexively threw her right arm out so hard that she nearly knocked the wind out of Margaret. She only barely managed to stop the car without crossing the black cat's trail.

Margaret began to cry. "I'm going to be late for my first day of school!"

Mother didn't answer, just chewed on a fingernail and stared at the patch of dirt in front of them. There was no way to get around the black cat's trail. No other way to get to school but this one. No place to turn around.

"Margaret, you know a person shouldn't cross a black cat's trail. *It's bad luck,*" Mother reminded.

"But I want to go to school!" Sniffles started to turn into hiccups.

No answer.

Then Mother, a grown woman who *knew* better, who had *certainly* been taught better by her *own* mother, did the unexpected. Tossing caution to the wind, she gunned the car's engine.

And drove right over that black cat's trail.

Back home, a penitent Mother confessed her foolish deed to Grandma. She could not explain what had gotten into her. She wrung her hands and wondered, *what had she been thinking?*

Grandma simply shook her head, gave Mother a hard look, and clucked worried disapproval.

There would be bad luck today.

Sure enough.

Within an hour, the phone rang.

Could someone pick Margaret up? There had been a little accident. While running on the playground, Margaret had tripped, fallen, and cut her lip on her lunch box. It was bleeding and might need stitches.

Mother and Grandma got their purses.

Later that evening, when a miserable, swollen-up, stitched-up-lipped-but-otherwise-in-one-piece Margaret developed a fever and broke out from head to toe with the chicken pox, neither Grandma nor Mother was surprised.

More bad luck.

But they *did* know what to do.

Mother and Grandma took Margaret outside, down to the barn, by the chicken coop. Margaret knew better than to cry or argue, but stumbled obediently along between them. At the coop, they told her to stand by the gate. Not to move. Then the two of them ran around and around the chicken yard, forcing the unhappy hens to flap their wings and fly crazily over and around Margaret's head.

"Takes the poison out of the pox," Grandma panted an explanation. "Don't worry. Won't hurt the hens at all."

This time no one was taking any chances.

Though her first day of school got off to a bad start, what with the black cat and the cut lip and the chicken pox and having to stand while the chickens flew over her head and all, Margaret did finally get to go. And just as she had expected, school was wonderful. So wonderful that she decided to spend her life there. Margaret became a teacher.

She and I met ten years ago when our sons played on the same Little League Baseball team. We became friends almost instantly. Unlike her mother and grandmother, Margaret did not believe in black cats and bad luck and such, but she did believe in the magic of friendship.

So did I.

We could talk for hours about *almost* anything. Since Margaret had a squeamish tummy, she was not at all interested in hearing about my work. "It's not all blood and guts," I'd playfully tell her. "There's also . . . " But she would hear *none* of it.

As for me, I *loved* to hear about *her* job teaching first grade. Margaret was a great storyteller, loved the kids in her class, and I could listen for hours to the tales she told of her students' hilarious antics.

But not all the stories Margaret told were funny.

She was almost in tears when she called me this evening.

"Have time to talk?" she asked.

"Sure. What's up?"

"Something happened at school today."

"What? Tell me."

Six-year-old Josh had come to school wet-eyed and red-nosed. Margaret pulled him aside. "What's the matter Josh? Have a rough morning?"

He nodded.

"Want to tell me about it?"

"Mommy ran over my kitty."

"I'm so sorry." Margaret cuddled him up. Wiped his tears. "I know you must feel very sad today. I love my kitty and I would feel sad if he got run over."

In a few minutes Josh returned to his seat. He seemed to feel better.

But Margaret watched him closely throughout the day. Though losing his kitty was certainly cause enough for Josh to feel bad, she wondered if there was something else wrong. All morning she noticed that whenever Josh would finish his work, would have a minute or two of free time, he would pull out his notebook and write. Very slowly and carefully . . . highly unusual behavior for a rambunctious first grade boy.

Finally, when the other kids went to lunch and Josh—so engrossed in his writing that he didn't hear the bell—stayed put, Margaret quietly moved close enough to read what he was writing.

> dear mommy plees let dady have 1 mor chans
> i miss dady
> plees, plees, plees let dady cum home
> luv Josh

Josh looked up.

Margaret did not speak. Couldn't for a moment. Finally, "that's a nice letter."

"I didn't know how to spell some of the words right. Teacher, could you correct my words so I can write it again? I want to spell all of the words right."

"Of course I will."

And so Margaret and Josh stayed in the classroom during lunch. It was a school no-no, but Margaret didn't care. She shared her sandwich with Josh and she corrected his letter and he wrote it over.

🦋

It is said that people hold on to superstitious beliefs because those beliefs give them a sense of power, make them feel as if they have at least *some* control over unpredictable, frightening, out-of-control events. It gives them some way to explain the unexplainable.

People need that.

Margaret understands. She needs it too. Every night before she goes to bed, Margaret spends a few minutes alone in her bedroom rocking chair. In the quiet of the darkness she reviews her day, thinks about her students, rejoices over their joys and their successes, grieves over their hurts and their difficulties.

Tonight, I know, she will be thinking about Josh. And she will wrestle and wrestle with how to explain the unexplainable.

But no matter how hard she tries, she won't be able.

And so tonight, like she does every single night, in the quiet of the darkness, my friend Margaret will bow her head and pray.

> *To you, O LORD, I lift up my soul;*
> *In you I trust, O my God.*
> PSALM 25:1,2

CHAPTER TWENTY-SIX

Sign of the Redbird

Even before she learned to read, Anna spent her Sunday afternoons pouring over furniture ads in the newspaper, studying and comparing competing stores' matching living room suite offerings. While other girls her age longed for Barbie cars and birthstone rings, Anna dreamed of sixty-piece sets of blue-flowered dishes. For years she cut out and collected shiny magazine advertisements for bathroom coordinates—ones where the toilet seats share the same clever motifs as the bath rugs, shower curtains, waste-baskets, and tissue box covers. On the way to school, she stared out the bus window and daydreamed about harvest gold washer and dryer sets.

When Anna was eighteen, she married Tim and they bought a house of their own. To Anna's disappointment, the real-life home and furnishings she shared with her husband never quite measured up to her well-coordinated girlhood dreams. Their newlywed budget allowed for few extras and his parents' hand-me-down furniture, even cleverly camou-flaged with matching sky blue slip covers, wasn't the same as a new showroom set. One of the plates from her wedding china got broken, and as a result, every time guests came for dinner someone had to eat off a piece of plain, white, every-day stoneware. And Anna became resigned to the fact that no matter how carefully one cares for them, pretty shower curtains always wear out months before their coordinated bath mats do.

But as a young wife she learned to relax and adjust. Anna was grateful that *one* part of her domestic life *did* turn out just as she'd planned. She and Tim produced four beautiful children in the perfect order: boy, girl, boy, girl. They had managed to space them, almost to the month, two years apart. Anna was particularly pleased with the well-thought-out names she'd chosen for her children.

"Mitchell, Margo, Mike, and Melissa," she'd recite when questioned about her offspring. "Two, four, six and eight years old." As they grew up and as Anne grew up too, she concluded that except for socks, it wasn't that important for things to match after all.

Sixteen years old, I was eager to make a good impression at my first job interview. Remembering my dad's coaching, I smiled and stuck out my hand and made direct eye contact. My prospective employer smiled back at me and I relaxed just a bit. Big mistake. *That* was when I dropped my purse on her foot. Like most teenagers, I carried *my life* around in that purse and it was heavy—five or six pounds at least. Mortified, I apologized profusely and scrambled to retrieve my scattered belongings.

The dignified, gray-haired shoe store owner, my interviewer, caught her breath, winced for only a moment, before recovering her composure and assuring me that her foot was fine. *Really.* Would I please sit down?

Despite my clumsy first impression, Anna, as she told me to call her, hired me on the spot to help out in her store. Working after school, Saturdays, and on school holidays, I learned to wait on customers, put up stock, straighten, and keep records. I loved the job.

And I loved Anna.

A tiny table tucked into a corner of the stock room held a coffee pot, mugs, and tins of cookies and crackers. When Anna discovered I didn't drink coffee, she brought packets of instant hot chocolate mix for me to sip during my break times. I heard her say she liked chocolate chip cookies, so I filled the cookie tin with a batch made from my mother's famous recipe.

Over the snack table hung a calendar, a two-week work schedule, and a chalkboard. Anna and I got into the habit of leaving surprise messages for each other. I started the ritual by printing on the chalkboard Philippians 1:3: *"I thank my God every time I remember you."* Anna was tickled to find the verse and in turn left a special message for me. We also clipped jokes and cartoons and taped them up for each other to find. I looked forward to coming to work, punching the time clock, and rushing to the back to see if Anna had left anything on the board for me.

For her birthday I gave Anna a funny card and a cluster of daisies wrapped up in green paper. At Christmas she presented me with a pair of racy, black, high-heeled sandals she'd watched me gaze longingly at for weeks.

I had worked at the shoe store for only a few weeks when I noticed that Anna collected redbirds. Her tote bag was decorated with redbirds, as was her umbrella, her notepad, and her favorite blouse. She owned a collection of redbird pins, and most days arrived at work with a gold-plated or red-enameled specimen perched on her shoulder or pinned to her collar.

"Anna," I asked one day over hot chocolate, "why do you like redbirds so much? When did you start collecting them?"

She smiled, took a sip of her coffee, and set her redbird-decaled mug down. "My children have always meant the world to me. When they were little we had such fun! Even when they were teenagers, we still had great times together.

And when they grew up, we stayed close." She paused. "Except for Mike."

This was the first time I'd heard Anna mention his name.

"Mike was my youngest son. After he finished high school, he started having lots of problems. His dad and I took him to our minister, to doctors, to therapists; tried to get him help. Mike was even on medication for awhile. But nothing we did seemed to work for very long. He was a sad young man."

I listened and let my cocoa grow cold.

"When Mike was twenty years old, he died suddenly." She paused and her voice became soft. "He walked out into the woods and killed himself."

She continued in a steady voice. "For years I was tormented with the way he died. I couldn't get it out of my mind. I couldn't find any peace. Every day I went to work, kept my house, played with my grandchildren, and tried to go on. But I was haunted by the way Mike died. Finally, I decided to ask God to let me know if he was okay."

I looked at her questioningly.

"I've always loved birds and I keep several feeders in my yard. My husband was a good-natured man, but he used to complain that the birds ate more cereal than all the rest of the family put together. I loved to see the different species that would come to the feeder. Outside my kitchen window I'd see birds of all sizes, colors, and varieties. Except for one. I was always disappointed that no matter what food I put out I never saw a single redbird. Ever. My friend across town had redbirds The neighbors down the street had redbirds. I even bought a special feeder designed to attract them. But it didn't help.

"So one day I was thinking about Mike and thinking about the birds and I got the idea to ask God for a redbird. I suppose it sounds crazy, but I prayed that if Mike was all right, *whatever that meant,* God would send a redbird to my yard. It would be a sign between me and Him. I prayed and I watched to see what would happen. And do you know that exactly one week later, on Mike's birthday..."

"You saw a redbird!" I interrupted.

Anna, shiny-eyed and grinning, corrected me, "not *a* redbird. A yard full! Maybe a hundred or more. In the trees, on the ground, at the feeders. The whole yard looked like the Red Sea."

I felt goose bumps pop up on my arms.

"The birds stayed around that whole day, but when I got up the next morning, they were gone. I've not seen another one in my yard since. So," she answered my question, "that's why I like redbirds. Whenever I see one I think of Mike."

Volumes have been written about what happens to someone like Mike when they die. There are wise folks and educated scholars who have studied long and hard and who are prepared to predict who among us will go to heaven and who won't.

I suppose there are just as many others among us who try very hard not to think about the subject. Because even among believers, a death like Mike's is a touchy subject, one most of us aren't comfortable talking about. We wrestle with it in private and we agonize over it and we still come up with many more questions than we do answers. Hard questions.

I certainly offer no answers.

All I know is that my friend Anna hasn't struggled with her son's sad death in a long time. She asked, and the reply she received was enough for her.

Today, whenever *I* see a redbird, I know it is for me too.

They will be a sign and a wonder to you.
DEUTERONOMY 28:46

PART FOUR

Time to Play

CHAPTER TWENTY-SEVEN

Only the Lonely

*L*ate last summer I received a welcome but unexpected and unscheduled-for writing assignment. The coveted surprise request came from a magazine that had, in fact, previously printed my unsolicited submissions. But this was the first time its publishers had asked me to produce a specific text for them. Since I am both an eager and aspiring writer, this request, at least in my mind, represented an important turning point in my relationship with the magazine. It told me that its time-pressured editors had enough faith in my abilities to trust me to write a specific, last-minute article for an upcoming issue.

I was thrilled.

My excitement was tempered by one small detail. The requested article needed to be written, spell-checked, edited, printed, and dropped into the U.S. Post Office's overnight mail slot within four working days.

Not a problem.

Usually.

In a crunch, I am able to write quickly, but this time, an added factor had to be to considered. That very afternoon, the afternoon I received the almost frantic editor's request, houseguests, dear friends from across the state, were expected to arrive for a week-long visit.

Still not a problem, I assured myself.

Once our guests, my friend Jeanna, her husband, Jack, and their two young children, were settled in, I explained the situation to them as nonchalantly as I could. We would still go to Astroworld (a nearby amusement park) the first day, have a picnic and swim in the lake at a local state park the next, and enjoy the zoo and a cookout the following day. There would be ample time to for us adults to catch up on family gossip, stroll in the woods, and play our traditional cut-throat, late-night card games. We would have a great time.

"I'll just need to take a teeny bit of time each day to work on my article," I told them.

"Of course," my friends assured me. "Don't mind us. Do what you need to do."

And so I did. I cooked breakfasts, washed towels, bought toilet paper, and refereed children's arguments. I chased the dog and fed the cat and blew up air mattresses. I made beds and emptied the trash and turned the TV down and made bowls of popcorn and pitchers of honey-sweetened iced tea.

And I made repeated unsuccessful attempts to steal a few minutes of solitude to write my article. I found it was all but impossible to orchestrate time alone with eight humans, a dog, and two cats all vying for personal space in our cottage-size home.

Still, though, I kept trying, and on the second afternoon of my friends' visit, the house fell quiet. I gleefully realized that all the adults in the house but me were napping or reading, while the kids were sprawled across the living room floor staring zombie-eyed at a rented video. I hurriedly popped a frozen chicken casserole into the oven, threw a Jell-O salad into the fridge, and almost disbelieving, dashed to our bedroom and sat down in front of the computer. If I could manage a couple hours of quiet, I reasoned, I could whip the majority of the piece right out. The necessary editing and correcting could easily be done in smaller snatches of time.

I turned on the computer and began to type. For two days, I'd been mulling over the article's format in my mind, so the words flowed easily. I was making good progress. Yes! I believed I was going to make my deadline after all.

About an hour had passed when Jeanna woke up. Feeling a bit lonely, she timidly knocked on the bedroom door. "Okay if I join you?"

"Sure. Come on in."

She stretched, yawned, and, leaving the door open, sprawled out on the bed behind my desk. Propping herself up on her elbows, she assured me, "I know you're working. I promise I'll be really quiet. Just let me read over your shoulder."

I was trying so hard to concentrate, my response to her was little more than an "uh huh."

Only a few minutes later Randy, tired of his magazine, ambled in to check out what we were doing. I guess we looked pretty interesting because he too stretched out on the bed.

He and Jeanna tried to be quiet. I really think they did, but their whispers and muffled laughter fell only inches from my ears. Still, attempting to ignore them, I pounded away at the keyboard.

When Jack woke up he felt left out and decided to join us. Finding no room on the bed and thinking it not a bit odd to find his wife lying in bed next to her friend's husband, he stretched out on the floor near my feet and absently began to drum a melodic rhythm on his knee. The moving percussion solo was interrupted only when Jack was tackled from behind by both his son and daughter. Ben and Sarah squealed and shrieked and begged for piggyback rides.

It was impossible for me to work. Defeated, I gave up. Stopped my frantic pecking. Took a deep breath. Turned around to face my interrupters.

The five of them froze.

"We're sorry," said Jeanna.

"We know you need to work," added Jack.

"We'll be quiet," chorused Ben and Sarah.

"Don't mind us," Randy assured me. "Do what you need to do."

I did.

I readily admit, it was I who delivered the first blow.

And the second.

Feathers flew.

It was the pillow fight to end all pillow fights.

No one really wants to be alone. Do they?

Except for a tattered, marked, and remarked family calendar, members of the Smith family would never have managed to show up at the right place on the right day this summer. Between church camp, summer jobs, a mission trip, visits with out-of-town family and friends, a Christian conference, and two cross-country car trips, the summer of '98 proved to be our busiest yet. And while I enjoyed every minute of the season's activities, by late July, true to my nature, I was eager for a bit of peace and quiet.

For while I love my husband and children, over the years I confess I've spent time wishing for something that just doesn't come with the maternal territory I've chosen. Many times, what I've craved, what I've longed for amidst the chaos of healthy family life, is time by myself. I am more than a bit uncomfortable when I admit how many times I've begged my family, both with words and desperate deeds, to leave me alone. For just for a few minutes. Please.

So I was quietly pleased when I realized that with our individual commitments, I would find myself home alone for five days and four nights in early August. I eagerly planned what I would do with this delicious gift of solitude: read and write and putter and sew. The house would be quiet and would stay tidy and I would have all the hot water I wanted and the whole bed to myself. The prospect sounded delicious.

And the first day it was. I listened to Handel instead of Hansen, and made molé instead of meatloaf. I splurged on three bottles of imported sparkling water and sat up late listening to Public Radio. It was great.

That day.

What I did not expect, what surprised me, was that just two days after my family members had scattered, I would find myself restless and out of sorts. It had sounded like a rare treat—having the house totally to myself for the first time in my 20-year marriage. But it didn't turn out to be nearly as much fun as I'd anticipated it to be. The house stayed tidy all right, but it also stayed quiet. Too quiet. Being an avowed TV-hater, I felt sheepish when I turned it on for the noise and the company.

After putting in half a day at my camp nurse job, instead of feeling productive and creative, I found myself sluggish and listless. I found it easy to fill my evenings with important tasks like reading stacks of out-of-date mail-order catalogues, repeatedly checking my email, and straightening the linen closet and silverware drawer.

I've never felt afraid at night, but once I crawled into bed, I heard all sorts of sounds I'd never noticed before. With no one to snuggle up next to, I was cold. Way too cold to sleep well, but not nearly cold enough to get up and adjust the thermostat. So instead of snoozing, I tossed and turned and wondered about my far-flung family. What were they doing? Were they in bed yet? Had they eaten? Were they having fun? I hoped so.

I missed them. A lot. Long hot showers are nice. A tidy house is great. And Public Radio has its place. But nothing, nothing beats the sound of car doors slamming, suitcases dropping, and shouts of "Hey Mom, we're home."

Especially when those sounds come a day early.

"We know you didn't expect us home until tomorrow," my husband explained. "But we finished up early and decided to drive on in."

"Don't mind us, Mom," my children assured me. "Do what you need to do."

And sweeping them up into big, smothering, mother-bear hugs, I did just that.

Leave her alone!
2 KINGS 4:27

CHAPTER TWENTY-EIGHT

A Star in My Eyes

My sister-in-law Martha is a bargain shopper extraordinaire. A master at gleaning amazing treasures from the most unlikely places, Martha rescues gourmet goodies from dusty, discount grocery store bins, claims classic, vintage accessories from thrift shop shelves, and plucks marked-below-cost clothing from the sale racks of exclusive department stores. Whether Martha wears it, serves it, gives it, or keeps it, you can bet she found it on sale.

Even though almost all of Martha's off-price purchases are good buys, she readily admits that occasionally she does make a mistake. Among her most memorable, not-quite-what-she-bargained-for treasures, found at a going-out-of-business downtown toy store, are two dozen packets of marked-down, glow-in-the-dark, self-sticking plastic stars—the kind designed to lend a celestial look to a child's bedroom ceiling.

What fun it would be, Martha thought, to surprise her sons (and my nephews), Tyler and Mason, with a bit of night-time sparkle. So she bought the stars. After the boys were asleep in their bunk beds, she stealthily crept into their shared bedroom, climbed up on a chair, and began adorning the ceiling with assorted sizes of the heavenly bodies. It took better than an hour to get them all up, and by the time she was finished, her neck was stiff and her arm ached. But the glow from the stars was as impressive as she'd hoped. Martha couldn't wait to wake the boys up, predawn, for school, and hear their excited reactions.

She was not prepared for what happened before morning. In the middle of the night, Mason and Tyler, asleep in their beds, felt something hit their faces. Drowsily, they brushed the somethings away. It happened again. And so again, they brushed away the nocturnal intrusions. Once more both boys felt something hit their faces. Finally, fully awake, Mason and Tyler sat up in their beds and rubbed their eyes. Above them, under, on them, and below them were stars, lots of stars, bargain stars backed with old, not-very-sticky adhesive, stars that were all in the process of turning loose and hurtling toward the carpet.

"Mom! Dad!" Tyler and Mason called. "Come quick! Hurry! Something's wrong. The sky is falling!"

Third-grader Mason is quite the basketball player. He loves to run and jump, dribble and shoot. He's pretty good—has some natural athletic ability, the coaches tell his parents. But there is one frustrating detail that Mason has had to learn about basketball. The game is a team sport, played by team members whose talents and abilities vary from day to day, game to game. In basketball, sometimes you win and sometimes you lose.

And this past season, Mason's team lost. A lot. All but one game, in fact. And it is not fun to lose.

Now my nephew is not a baby. He is not one to throw a tantrum or pitch a fit. But after his team came in dead last, again, at a recent all-day Saturday tournament . . . well it was just too much. When the first place team, the second place team, the third place team, and even the fourth place team were awarded big shiny trophies, when the players who received the trophies began to strut around the gym and shout their victory chants, neither he nor his downcast team members were able to hide their frustration and disappointment.

Their mothers, huddled together in the bleachers, watched it all and commiserated over their sons' bruised egos.

"Our boys played hard," Steven's mother said.

"They did their best," Martha agreed.

"They were good sports," Adam's mom added.

"Couldn't have played any harder," asserted Matthew's mother.

"Shouldn't they get some recognition too? After all, winning isn't everything is it?" voiced Sam's mom.

"Of course it's not!" the mothers agreed in unison. "Let's do something special for them too. They deserve it!"

And so the mothers hatched a plan. They would take charge of organizing an end-of-the season celebratory picnic. Hot dogs would be roasted, cupcakes baked, and fruit punch poured. And, to every boy who had played, both the winners and the losers, the mothers would give an identical trophy. The trophies, engraved Star Participant, would be presented with great ceremony and fanfare.

The boys, their boys especially, the mothers knew, would be thrilled with the unexpected honors.

And, on the sunny day of the hot dog supper, when the trophies were handed out, some of the boys were.

Thrilled, that is.

Not Mason.

Martha was embarrassed when she had to make him go back and say thank you to the woman who had presented the trophies. And instead of examining his prize, instead of waving it proudly over his head like the other boys were doing, Mason shoved his into his gym bag.

"Mason," Martha asked impatiently, "what's wrong? Don't you like the trophy? Aren't you proud of it?" She and the other team mothers had gone to a lot of trouble to raise the money to buy the trophies, had counted and recounted to be sure they had ordered enough, and had made two out-of-town trips to pick them up.

He did not answer.

"Mason, I'm talking to you! Show me your award. Let me see it."

Reluctantly he retrieved the trophy and handed it to Martha.

"It's very nice. I'm proud of you."

He would not look at her or at the trophy.

Once at home, Martha lectured Mason about his ungrateful behavior, about how he didn't even seem to appreciate his award.

"But Mom," he finally explained. "It doesn't mean anything. You get a trophy because you earn it, not just because someone gives it to you."

Ouch.

Martha saw her mistake at once. She and the other mothers had certainly meant well, had only been trying to make the boys feel good about themselves, had sought to make them happy. But Mason was right. What good was an award if a person hadn't earned it?

Mason interrupted her thoughts. "Mom, don't worry. Me and Matthew were talking. We're going to practice and practice and practice, and next year we think we'll be really good. Really, really good, Mom. Just wait. We'll get a BIG trophy next year. We'll earn it."

❧ ❧

Martha and Dayne recently remodeled their house to give the family a larger living room and Mason and Tyler separate bedrooms. In preparation for the boys moving into their new rooms, Martha spent a weekend sorting through their dresser drawers, their desks, their closets, and their shelves, putting items into one of three sacks: Stuff to Keep, Stuff to Store, and Stuff to Throw Away. She came across all sorts of childhood memorabilia—odd puzzle and game pieces, mismatched and outgrown athletic socks, school papers and old report cards. On the bottom of a dusty pile, in the back corner of Mason's closet, Martha came upon the scorned Star Participant trophy and a long-forgotten, glow-in-the-dark, plastic ceiling star.

Martha did not hesitate before tossing the trophy into the Stuff to Throw Away bag. The star, however, took a bit longer. She studied it, wiped at the dust and lint that was stuck to the back of it, held it up to the light. She smiled when she remembered the night the stars had fallen on Mason's head.

Finally, she decided to throw it away too.

I think Martha made the right decision about the star. It was just plastic. And who needs a fake, stick-on celestial body when you have living, breathing, jumping, sweating, dribbling, and shooting Mason right in the same house with you?

Because even without a trophy, I think my nephew Mason will always be a real star.

Humility comes before honor.
Proverbs 15:33

CHAPTER TWENTY-NINE

Salt, Butter, Coffee, and a Corset

I can only remember seeing Granny Hill sick one time. Someone had brought her a paper sack full of fresh, garden-grown, ripe tomatoes. There may have been a half dozen tomatoes in that sack, but hidden behind the closed door of her nursing home bedroom, Granny had salted and eaten every one of them like she was munching on sweet apples.

Made a pig of herself, she did, knowing that they would make her sick.

And sick she was. Rolling around on her bed, groaning and clenching her stomach. The sight of her fragile, less-than-five-foot frame in such agony frightened me. I feared she might even be dying until someone explained, "She gets this way every time she eats tomatoes. Can't help herself. Loves them so much that she goes ahead and eats them anyway. She'll be all right by morning."

And miraculously she was.

Only a few years later, on the eve of Granny Hill's one-hundredth birthday, I quizzed her. "What's your secret,

Granny? How have you managed to live so long and stay so active?"

She gave me a quick grin and a wicked wink. "You really want to know? Really? Then you better write this down."

I complied. Got out paper and pen. "Go ahead. I'm ready."

"Eat a lot of salt."

"Salt?"

"Put lots of butter on your bread."

"Real butter?"

"Drink at least a pot of coffee every morning."

"A whole pot?"

"And wear a good stiff corset every day. Every day." She stressed.

She was serious.

Some folks wait until well into their old age to gain a little feistiness, to cut loose a bit. Not Granny Hill. Set down in the middle of a pack of five children—four girls and one boy— Granny was born looking at the world with different eyes. Unlike her feminine, ladylike sisters who learned early to embroider and crochet, to cook and to can, Granny learned to milk cows and ride horses and build fences and jump creeks.

As a young child she was mischievous, energetic, and fearless. Once, when no one was looking, Granny climbed to the top of the windmill to see how it worked. She looked around, felt the wind on her face, and stuck her index finger into the workings of the elevated machine just to find out what would happen. The bloody results of her experimentation left her with a scarred, mangled, and crooked finger that she put to creative good use every chance she got. All three of her sisters were sissy, silly, goosey-type girls and Granny had great fun making scary faces and menacing sounds while chasing them around the room, threatening to touch them with her ugly finger.

"Ma-ma," they'd tattle and cry.

"She's pointing her evil finger at us again!"

"Make her stop."

"Make her leave us alone!"

Granny would just laugh and hiss and wag that infamous finger at them some more.

Tradition was that every year, on Granny's mid-May birthday, the whole family would pack a picnic lunch, load up into the horse-drawn wagon, and go berry picking. And on that day—always on Granny's birthday and not one day before—in an important annual outdoor ceremony, she and her siblings would be allowed to shed their heavy socks and cumbersome lace-up shoes and go barefoot. No matter how balmy the April and early May weather might happen to be on a given year, no matter how much they begged and pleaded, not until Granny's birthday were the children allowed to go barefoot.

It was on the occasion of her ninth birthday when, after an hour-long wagon ride, and after she and her brother and sisters had gleefully pulled off their socks and shoes and piled them into the back of the wagon, that Granny admitted to feeling a little bit ill. Her mama felt her head and looked at her tongue, but she found no discernable sign of serious illness.

Everyone was eager to get on with the berry picking; was at that very moment engaging in sweet-toothed daydreams of the berry pies Mama would make for supper. So Papa spread out a quilt and made Granny a soft pallet on the grass under the wagon. She could rest there while the rest of them picked. They would be close by and if she needed anything she could call for someone.

Fine. Granny, really more tired than sick, and to be honest, not at all in the mood to pick berries, drifted off to sleep. When she awoke, she found two buckets of berries next to her. As her brother and sisters and mama and daddy had filled buckets, they had tiptoed back to the wagon and set their precious plunder in the shade under the wagon.

Granny was suddenly hungry. Starving. And so she helped herself to a few berries. First she ate one. Then two. Then three. And finally she began scooping handfuls of berries into her mouth, chewing and swallowing as fast as she could. They tasted so good!

And so it was to a very sick little girl and to a pair of almost empty berry buckets that her family returned. Granny had eaten the better part of two gallons of the wild fruit. Early in the season as it was, only a few berries had been ripe and so two buckets full were about all the fruit the family had been able to pick.

It was a long ride home. No one in the wagon, their dreams of berry pies dashed al! to pieces, was terribly sympathetic to Granny's aching and bulging tummy. In fact, not one of her sisters would even speak to her till the next day.

🐦 🐦

My friend Katie is Granny Hill's granddaughter. She tells me that in spite of her rude and unruly childhood behavior, Granny grew up to be the kindest, gentlest, most unselfish woman she's ever known. Best of all, Granny never lost her love of fun and Katie has wonderful memories of good times spent with Granny.

Katie has tried to carry on some of Granny Hill's traditions. She thinks of Granny every time she sees a windmill and every time that, while she's picking wild berries for pies, she eats a few from her bucket.

Katie never, ever, let her children go barefoot before Granny's birthday. No matter how much they begged and pleaded. To do so just wouldn't seem right.

Granny passed away a few years ago. She had one of the biggest funerals anyone around the community can remember. The minister read her favorite Scripture, an old-time gospel group crooned her favorite songs, and some old friends told of how they would remember her.

When mourners walked past Granny Hill's casket they couldn't tell, but might have guessed, that under her church dress she was wearing a good stiff corset. What they could see however, were the goodies tucked in next to Granny: a can of coffee, a box of salt, and a pound of butter.

The casket perishables made quite an impression on those who attended Granny's funeral. People talked. And everyone chuckled and agreed they will never forget what Granny claimed were the secrets of a long life.

But just in case anyone does forget, I tell them not to worry—for I have them all written down.

He will renew your life
and sustain you in your old age.
RUTH 4:15

CHAPTER THIRTY

Fruit and Flowers

The cynical among us annually inform the rest of us that Mother's Day is just a scheme set up to make money for the phone companies, the florists, and the folks who print greeting cards. I suppose these helpful individuals could be believed, but at the same time, I don't think it was a mother who spoke those words of disrespect about what most females view as a perfectly good holiday. Every mother I know loves cards and calls and candy and presents, and quite honestly, I've yet to meet a woman with any deep-seated objections to being pinned with a corsage and taken out to eat after church.

Billy's mom is no exception. Over the years she's come to look forward to, in fact to expect that she will have a big, fancy, ribbon-bedecked, double orchid pinned to her chest and be taken out to eat at her favorite Chinese restaurant on a certain sunny Sunday in May.

And her only son, Billy, has yet to disappoint her. Even though his mama now lives in a nursing home, has to take medicine, and gets around in a wheelchair, she says that the take-out, salty fried rice and tangy sweet-and-sour pork Billy brings her for Mother's Day lunch tastes almost as good as the restaurant meals she used to enjoy. And since Billy is among the faithful volunteers who show up each week to hold a special senior citizen service in the nursing home's tiny carpeted chapel, she still gets to wear a showy corsage to church on Sunday.

And so it was no surprise when, bright and early on Mother's Day Sunday, Billy showed up at the nursing home with a plastic florist box wrapped with a shiny silver ribbon. He was running a bit late and so his mama was waiting in the chapel when he arrived. No matter. The service hadn't started and he strode right in and pinned that pretty corsage on her.

She hugged him and kissed him and beamed like sunshine.

Billy took a hymn book, straightened his tie, and took a seat next to her. He had been coming to the home to help with the services for more than ten years. Every week he helped wheel elderly worshipers to and from the chapel, often led the closing prayer, and once a month delivered a stirring ten-minute sermonette. Over the years he'd grown to know and love the thirty or so residents, mostly widowed women, who attended each week. Billy knew who among the little flock had been ill, who enjoyed frequent visitors, and who had practically no surviving relatives.

The service opened with a prayer and a hymn. Billy's mama reached up and touched her corsage, smiled at him, and patted his arm. He squeezed her hand, then glanced around. None of the other ladies, though decked out in their Sunday best, wore corsages. Their bosoms remained unadorned. And though he tried to concentrate on the sermon, on the prayers, and on the hymns, throughout the worship service he caught women looking at his mama's pretty flower. Several times the women's admiring eyes would accidentally meet his. They would smile shyly and look back at their hymn books.

Distracted, Billy glanced at his watch and shifted in his seat.

Billy's granddad Poppy was famous in three counties for the good watermelons he grew. Out of the rich and sticky, black-land earth of his north Texas farm, Poppy coaxed forth the sweetest, juiciest fruits a person's lips and chin could ever hope to sink into. Red-meated ones and yellow-meated ones, small, dark-skinned, round varieties, and elongated, light-striped ones grew in vine-tangled abundance under the hot sun in Poppy's well-fertilized, back forty watermelon patch.

During the summer, while Poppy watered and hoed and hand-picked the melons, his wife, aided by a grandkid or two, peddled them from a tin-roofed roadside stand situated just off the interstate that ran between Dallas and Texarkana. They enjoyed a good trade from the locals as well as from a steady stream of out-of-county tourists, most of whom were ignorantly happy to pay highly inflated prices.

"City folks don't know no better," Poppy confided to the grandkids.

Because of their predictable goodness, seldom did Poppy find himself with more watermelons than could be sold from the stand. But on the rare occasion when an overabundance of the fruit threatened to become overripe, when they were within a day or two of losing that musical, mystical, just-ripe, tell-tale thud when thumped, Poppy loaded them into the back of his rusty black pick-up truck and hauled them to town. He would never, ever, knowingly sell an overripe watermelon—even at a reduced price. "A man," he sternly instructed his grandkids, "can never be too careful about his reputation."

A shrewd businessman, Poppy waited until evening to set out to sell the melons because by then most all the menfolk were home. "Hardworking men, once they've come in, washed up, and pulled their boots off, are especially likely to crave, to have their teeth set, for the taste of a good sweet watermelon," Poppy would explain to the grandkids.

So about six o'clock or so, he would draft his oldest grandboy, Billy, and together in the truck they would creep up and down the dusty streets of the town's poorest neighborhoods (experience had taught Poppy that poor folks just seem to eat watermelons better than rich folks do), blowing the truck horn and hawking the yet-unsold produce. Poppy drove and Billy, slump-shouldered and obedient but to-the-bone tired, would perch on the open tailgate of the truck, his lanky, twelve-year-old legs hitting the dirt every time the truck hit a low spot in the street. Up and down Poppy steered, while Billy hollered, "Wah-termelons, waaah-termelons! Come and git your WAAAH-termelons."

And always, people came out of their houses, off of their front porches, and around from their back yards to buy Poppy's watermelons. He sold them for fifty cents apiece. From the folks who couldn't afford fifty cents, he would take twenty-five cents for half a melon.

When someone asked for a half, Poppy pulled up to the customer's yard, laid the chosen melon on the tailgate of the pickup, and with one swift swipe of a butcher knife, hacked the fruit in two. He would then take a step back, avert his eyes, and graciously allow the customer to choose the half he wanted to buy.

Once the half melon was paid for, Poppy and Billy would sit on the customer's front stoop, would borrow the customer's own salt shaker to season their portion, and eat the other half themselves. They might be at a widow woman's house and be sharing the porch with six rusty-necked kids fighting over thin slivers of the half melon their mama had bought for them. And Billy and Poppy might already be full as ticks from eating unsold watermelon halves, but that made no difference to Poppy. He—and at his insistence, Billy—ate the other half.

Only once, feeling bloated and ill after eating his share of three half melons, did Billy ask Poppy why they didn't just give the customer the other half.

"Wouldn't be right," Poppy spoke between bites. "Folks get what they pay for. If they pay for a half, they should get a half."

◦⅌ ⅁◦

It has been said that the apple never falls far from the tree, but I don't believe that bit of so-called wisdom for a minute. If you care to challenge my view, pay a visit to the sweet-faced, stiff-jointed, gray-headed attendees of a certain weekly nursing home church service. You'll be welcome there any Sunday, but try to go on Mother's Day. Pick up a hymnal and find a seat in the middle of a row of pretty ladies.

Once you are settled, ask them, any one of them, "Where did you get such a lovely corsage?"

"We don't know," will be their mysterious reply. "They're from someone called anonymous. We get them every year. All of us. Aren't they pretty?"

Once the service is over, stay for lunch. There is sure to be plenty. The menu of the day might not be what you'd expect for a senior citizen Sunday dinner, but don't worry. If you're not fond of fried rice and sweet-and-sour pork, you can fill up on dessert.

It will be the sweetest, juiciest watermelon you've ever put in your mouth.

A gift opens the way for the giver
and ushers him into the presence of the great.
PROVERBS 18:16

CHAPTER THIRTY-ONE

No Green Turtlenecks

My friend Joni and I perch obediently in our assigned seats at a candle-lit, dress-up banquet. We munch on our salads and pick at our chicken and feign appropriate interest in the evening's well-prepared but uninspiring speaker. "Love your dress," I whisper between bites. "It's gorgeous. That color makes your eyes look even bluer than they are."

"Goodwill," she mouths back at me.

A week later, Joni and I are together again, this time on a family camping trip. I'm shivering in last year's bulky-but-not-very-warm cotton jacket. Usually more cold-natured than I, this foggy morning Joni slowly sips her coffee. She appears relaxed and toasty in a lightweight navy blue parka I've never seen her wear before.

"Is that jacket down-filled?" I ask between teeth chatters.

"Yep. Got it yesterday at the Salvation Army thrift store. Cost seven dollars."

Sunday morning, my husband and children are out of town so Joni and I meet for coffee before church. She is picking the colored sprinkles off her chocolate glazed donuts and I'm admiring her red suit. "New outfit?"

"Uh huh. Found it at a garage sale. Still had the tags on it."

Joni buys all her clothing secondhand. And most of her shoes. Partly because of her thriftiness, she is realistically planning to quit her job next month and live on her savings and investments. She's not sure what she'll do long term, but for the next six months, she's going to live in Mexico and work at an orphanage. Once she gets there, Joni plans on washing clothes, mopping floors, and scrubbing toilets. And hopefully, rocking a few babies. Hopefully.

It is a mystery to me how Joni manages to live contentedly with so few material possessions. The child of an alcoholic, out-of-control, and, thankfully, mostly absentee father, she grew up poor. Neither she nor her five brothers and sisters possessed the clothes or toys or books other kids had.

Her family moved often and it was embarrassing for Joni to repeatedly be the new kid in a new class, to forever be behind in her lessons, and to never be dressed quite right. Junior High was the worst. Her mother and dad were apart for most of those three years, so they camped with an aunt and an uncle in a trailer house full of baby cousins.

Adolescent poverty was obvious in girls who dressed poorly and in boys who rarely possessed the proper school supplies. It was felt by siblings who sat together in the school cafeteria and kept their heads low. And it was literally tasted by students who choked down government free lunch Salisbury steaks and green beans, pretending not to notice classmates who bought and often didn't even finish paper-wrapped cheeseburgers and salty french fries.

Though Joni and her brothers and sisters often felt alone and singled out in their deprivation, they weren't. Other kids lived in similar situations, in families headed by fathers without jobs, by mothers who took in pennies-a-piece ironing, by grandparents who struggled to support houses full of hungry grandchildren on meager monthly pension checks.

Joni knew some of her teachers felt sorry for them—for the "poor" kids. She realized that anonymous members of the community tried to help them. The do-gooders meant well but their pity, their secret sacks of mothball-smelling, hand-me-down clothing and packages of free pencils and notebook paper, only embarrassed her and her siblings.

Each Christmas Joni's family, along with other local low-income households, received a holiday box. They were delivered on Christmas Eve, house-to-house with great festive fanfare by enthusiastic members of local charities. Inside the cardboard containers families would find the makings for a Christmas dinner with all the trimmings, two rolls of toilet paper, an unwrapped bar of soap, an assortment of plastic combs, and a clear sack of peppermint candy. There would also be a wrapped present for each child in family. The packages held no mystery, for each year they concealed the very same item. As predictable as the frozen turkeys and the cans of cranberry sauce, every child, every year, received the generous gift of an itchy, army green turtleneck sweater.

Joni guessed they bought them by the case.

And every year her mother, as if bound by some secret agreement with every other poverty-stricken, box-receiving mother in town, would make—no, would force her children to wear the green sweaters on the first day of school after the Christmas holidays. No amount of begging or pleading would change her mind, nor the mind of any of the other mothers. Insisting that their offspring wear the charity turtlenecks was an expected sign of gratitude, a nonverbal acknowledgement of thanks, an assurance that there would be future Christmas boxes.

And so, the first Monday after New Year's Day would find runny-nosed kindergartners, gawky fourth graders, hunch-shouldered junior highers, and even stony-faced high schoolers wearing matching sweaters. In every classroom, there would be three or four or maybe a half-dozen kids, itching and miserable in their army green turtlenecks.

In case there had been any doubt in anyone's mind up until that time, thanks to the boxes of holiday cheer, now the whole world knew which kids were charity cases.

❧ ❧

I arrive at Joni's house to pick her up for a concert. We are having girls' night out tonight, and predictably, I am early and she is not yet home from work. Though it is late fall, the weather is nice and I've been inside all day so I decide to get out and wait on her front porch. I climb her steps and am surprised to see five large cardboard boxes stacked next to the front door. The boxes bear the return address of a well-known mail order clothing distributor. Must be a mistake, I muse. Joni would never order new clothes. Five boxes? But I take a closer look and see the boxes are indeed addressed to Joni.

She drives up.

"Hey girl," I tease and point at the boxes. "I see you ordered yourself a new wardrobe. Get anything for me?"

She looks sheepish. "It's just some things for the Christmas boxes the town gives away. You know, turtlenecks."

"Turtlenecks?" I question. She unlocks and I help her drag the boxes inside.

Together we kneel on the carpet and open the cartons with kitchen knives. Inside I see there are indeed turtlenecks. Soft cotton ones. Dozens of turtlenecks in each box. There are sky blue ones, brilliant purple ones, sunshine yellow ones, pale pink ones, and fire engine red ones. There are striped ones, paisley print ones, flowered ones, and plaid ones.

"I had no idea turtlenecks came in all these colors," I say, amazed. Offhandedly, I comment, "I don't see any green ones."

"Nope, no green ones. Couldn't find a single one." She avoids my eyes.

"Too bad," I say.

"Yes," she agrees with a wicked smile. "Too bad."

> *I needed clothes and you clothed me.*
> MATTHEW 25:36

CHAPTER THIRTY-TWO

Everything in Its Place

A trio of brass and wood plaques proclaiming the notable pie-baking abilities of three generations of females hangs on the wall in my mom's kitchen. It was first my mother, then I, and finally my pre-teen daughter who captured "Best of Show" in the pie and pastry contest category at our county's annual fair. Good cooking comes as naturally to my family's women as playing musical instruments or excelling in sports might come to yours.

What does not come easily to we three pie-bakers is housekeeping. We agree with our friend Karey, who says that a spotlessly clean house is the sure sign of a boring woman.

You may find dust bunnies and old newspapers in my mother's living room, stumble over baskets of clothes waiting to be folded in my house, and find it difficult to take three cautious steps into my daughter's cluttered bedroom. But stick with us and, rest assured, you will be well-fed and you will not be bored.

My mom paints and draws, sews her own clothes, and is teaching herself to speak both Spanish and Swahili. My daughter plays basketball, leads cheers, acts in plays, and swims every chance she gets. I write and speak, stencil, craft, and collect.

All of us are voracious readers and all of us love to go. Anywhere. Like eager, tail-wagging canines, just open the car door and we're in. Front seat, back seat, window seat, or middle, we are always ready for the next adventure.

So who, we wonder, has time for housekeeping?

Our husbands, Louie and Randy, gratefully have high dirt tolerances and assure us they'd choose fun over order any day. Once I bemoaned to my loyal but super-clean friend Sheri the horrible state of my house. I'd not cooked a decent meal in weeks, I told her, and neither of my kids had any clean underwear. I was writing day and night, struggling to meet a fast-approaching deadline.

Gently, very gently, sweet Sheri asked if perhaps I was neglecting my family.

Later that day, I repeated our conversation to my husband Randy. "Tell me," I implored, "honestly. Am I neglecting what I should be doing? Should I forget this project and take better care of you guys?"

Randy's indignant, chest-swelled response was immediate: "Annette, you tell anyone who asks, that you may be neglecting your house but you're not neglecting your family!"

I love that guy.

So everyone seems to be happy with us the way we are.

There is only one unexplainable glitch in this genetic legacy of haphazard housekeeping. When planning to be away from home for an extended length of time—say three nights or more—my mother and I are overcome with the need to put our surroundings in order. Perfect order. Maybe it's the irrational fear of something happening to us and our tidy friends and well-kept family members finding our houses in embarrassing disarray when they arrive for the wake. Understandably, dirty dishes in our ovens and ten-year-old mail-order catalogues in our guest bathrooms are not what we want mentioned in our eulogies.

No matter what our destination, we begin every out-of-town trip sore-muscled and red-eyed from staying up most of the previous night cleaning. We scrub and shine and dust and wipe. We fold and iron and bleach and stack. And most curious of all, we tend our houseplants. Our most pitiful ivies and most bedraggled ferns, ignored and unwatered for weeks, must be pruned, fed, and thoroughly saturated before we can even think about leaving home. I suppose we don't want the ladies from our churches, the faithful ones who would come to tend our families should we meet tragic out-of-town demises, to discover how truly neglectful and disorganized we were.

Last Christmas, my husband received a fancy, expensive power screwdriver. Top-of-the-line, the impressive tool featured multiple interchangeable heads and an ergonomically-designed handle. Randy was understandably proud of the gift and determined to take good care of it.

There was just one problem. We are not "tool people." Though a nice red-enameled box sits on a shelf in our garage, its contents include no tools, unless you count duct tape, crochet yarn, and a plastic Mickey Mouse pencil sharpener. It's not that we never need or use tools. We do. We just can't ever find them.

So obviously, the tool box was not even considered as a possible home for Randy's valuable gift. Where should he put it? The kitchen drawers were all full, and the VCR cabinet didn't seem like a fitting place. It wouldn't wedge into our already crammed bedside table, and the shoe box holding my counted cross-stitch patterns didn't seem secure enough. Then, brilliantly, Randy decided to stash the new tool in his sock drawer. Surely one of the safest places in our home.

But no, it too, was full.

So, settling for his second choice, he lovingly laid his new power screwdriver to rest in my panty drawer.

My friend Lee Ann and her sister Charlotte, both ministers' wives, have made a pact with each other. Should something happen to either of them, such as sudden death or incapacitation, the other will rush over and empty out the remaining sister's lingerie drawer. They know that their grandmother, an organized, industrious woman, would surely take it upon herself to, within hours, help a bereaved grandson-in-law by sorting and storing his departed wife's clothing. And, to state it plainly, grandmother would be shocked at the garments she would find in her granddaughter's nightie drawers. Grandmother, the sisters fear, might have a stroke.

It's not that Lee Ann and Charlotte don't appreciate the ruffled flannel nightgowns and tailored cotton pajamas Grandmother gives them every birthday, they just don't wear them.

Ever.

Which troubles neither of their happy husbands.

Learning of their efficient plan reminds me of my own dilemma. Before leaving town, I can be sure my house is in order and my plants are green and healthy. I am reasonably certain nothing is growing in my refrigerator, and I leave my children with enough clean clothes to last a season. I believe I have those areas well-covered. But one thing I have yet to figure out. If I died unexpectedly, would the church ladies—the ones who love and respect me now—ever come to grips with finding mechanical objects in my underwear drawer?

I fear they would never think of me the same way again.

❧ ❧

All of us wish to be well-remembered when we die. We want our loved ones to recall good things about us, to dwell on the times we were kind and loving and gracious. And likewise, we hope time erases their memories of occasions when we were impatient and selfish, times when we should have held our tongues instead of letting them run loose.

I know housekeeping and plant-watering and stacks of laundry matter little in the scheme of my life. They will be of no concern when I'm gone. And so I try every day, some days more successfully than others, to live in a way that will leave behind good memories for my husband and children. They, not friends or distant relatives or even helpful church ladies, are the ones who matter most to me.

Yet I am human, and just in case, since I am going out of town next week, and since I don't have a sister, I think I'll start looking for some other place to keep my undergarments.

Someplace far, far away from my husband's power tools.

I hope to visit you while passing through.
Romans 15:24   •

CHAPTER THIRTY-THREE

Perfect Landing

I stand in line, nervously digging my bare feet into the white sand, fiddling with my sunglasses, waiting for my turn. For several summers I've been coming with my family to this peaceful, oceanside, Florida vacation spot. And year after year, I have found myself enviously watching as daredevil parasailers soared high above the earth. I have watched as these normal-looking folks allow themselves—pay money in fact—to be strapped to parachutes, tethered to motor boats, and towed out over the ocean.

But, though I have thought about trying it, have secretly even dreamed of experiencing it, until this moment I have never even come close to actually doing it.

Then quickly, surprisingly quickly, the line dissipates and it is my turn. After signing a legal consent form, I am strapped between my knees, around my waist, and over my shoulders with heavy leather harnesses. My helper and instructor, a young woman, deeply-tanned and bikini-clad, is patient with my awkwardness, seems not to think it odd that I, in my matronly, wide-strapped, skirted swimsuit, stand among thrill seekers half my age.

I am grateful for her polite indifference.

This is to be our last day of vacation. The four of us—Mom, Dad, son, Russell, and daughter, Rachel, have made memories to last. We swam in the ocean, sunned on the sand, played rounds and rounds of cut-throat miniature golf, and competed in lazy games of spades. We feasted on hot dogs and ice cream and on extra-spicy french fries. And on this, our last evening, while dining on fresh-caught seafood at a dazzling, reef-top restaurant, we were the lucky audience for a group of dolphins putting on an impromptu show.

It was a great vacation week—one of the best, we four agree, and on this last day we find ourselves tired, a bit sunburned, and waterlogged, but relaxed and satisfied. In twelve hours, we will be packed and headed toward Texas, having completely spent both the time and money allotted for our yearly sabbatical.

As we travel the winding beachside road from the restaurant back to our rented condo, no one in the car speaks. The drive is smooth and hypnotic and we are lost in our own thoughts, gazing out the open windows at the waves, the gulls, and the soon-to-be-setting sun. My eyes stay fixed on the tiny parasailing figures, most of them tourists just like us, as their legs dangle and their arms wave, suspended from brilliantly-colored red, blue, and purple air-filled canopies.

Once, early in the week, I offhandedly mentioned to Randy that parasailing looked like fun to me. So fearful of heights that his feet begin to ache if he steps beyond the third rung of a stepladder, he had not had much to say about my interest. I was not sure Randy had even heard me, so neutral was his mumbled reply.

So I did not mention it again. At $50 a ride, parasailing was much too expensive to consider. It would be frivolous to spend that amount of money on an experience so fleeting, especially one only I would enjoy.

Truthfully, I wasn't sure I had the courage to try it anyway. But during that last evening's drive to the condo, Randy interrupted my thoughts. "Were you serious about wanting to go parasailing?"

"Not really," I hedge.

"If you want to, this is your chance. We still have time today. We can go right now," he offers.

I make excuses. "We don't have money left for it. It's getting late. We should be getting back so we can start packing up. Maybe next year," still unable to move my eyes from the tiny figures.

"I want to go parasailing," volunteers the teenage son.

"Me too," exclaims the daughter.

"Nope," Dad intervenes. "Just your mom. If she wants to." He steers the car onto the beach, drives directly to the parasail take-off area, pulls into a parking spot, and kills the engine. "Here's your chance. Do you want to or not?"

Do I?

My palms sweat.

My heart races.

"I do."

While I'm being strapped in, Randy hands over the cash. The children bounce up and down in the sand.

"Mommy, you're going to be up so high," giggles Rachel.

"I can't believe you're doing this." Russell is impressed.

"Have fun," and a quick kiss from Randy.

I'm in position, motorboat in front of me, parachute trailing behind me. Tethered to both, I hear the engine rev up. A whistle blows. As instructed, I take three running steps. Almost. On the third step, I trip and fall. An instant of panic, disappointment, humiliation. Quickly though, I'm plucked from my knees, straight up it seems, into the air. I'm propelled by the boat, lifted by the parachute above me.

My senses are overwhelmed. The sight from up so high is vast, unlike anything my brain can reference. Wind caresses my bare legs and the smell of the ocean fills my head. There is incredible silence. I am unable to hear a single human voice. And I am unable to make myself heard.

I am alone.

And it is wonderful.

My few moments in the air were both exhilarating and terrifying and exciting and awful. I don't expect to ever do it again. Parasailing was for me, a once-in-a-lifetime, wouldn't-miss-it-for-the-world, but don't-want-to-do-it-again experience. The memory of it—the sensation of coming as close to flying as I imagine a person ever can—is one I will treasure forever.

There have been other times in my life when I wanted to fly, when I felt the urge try something new, to take a risk, to meet some outlandish challenge. But because I am a wife, and a mom, and because we wives and moms are responsible and reliable, sacrificial and selfless, I held back on trying what my heart so desired.

Some of those times it would have been impractical or inconvenient to follow my unconventional dreams. But on other occasions, I simply found a safe place to hide—a place directly behind my domestic duties.

I offered them as excuses:

"Who would watch the kids?"

"I'd get home too late."

"We shouldn't spend the money."

Often, too often, I was simply afraid to try.

This afternoon, as I write about that day on the beach, referred to in family history as The Day Mom Went Parasailing, I remember the tiniest details of what I saw, what I heard, how it felt. I recall the smell of the ocean, the feel of the breeze on my bare legs and the sun on my back, the sight of my husband and my children waving as I rise from their sight.

And then I get to the part I remember best about the whole experience.

The boat slows and I drift over the beach. Lower and lower I sink. I can hear my children cheering and I'm close enough to see the green-around-the-mouth look of relief on my husband's face. My feet hit the sand and I shrug off the harnesses and I feel their arms tighten around me.

"Way to go, Mom!"

"Was it fun, Mommy?"

"I'm glad you made it back okay. Want to go again?"

I hug them back and straighten my swimsuit straps and I look in their faces and I know, at that moment, that I do not need to be afraid.

I have no need to hide.

I am safe.

And it's okay to dream.

I said, "Oh, that I had the wings of a dove!"
Psalm 55:6

CHAPTER THIRTY-FOUR

Bright and Shiny

*M*atthew was an unhappy baby from the start. Nothing—not a perfectly warmed bottle of formula, not a soft cuddly blanket, not even the moon and stars mobile his Aunt May made for him—made him happy. He cried at intervals throughout the day and slept in little more than thirty-minute spurts at night. Matthew, when only a few weeks old, acted jittery. Nervous even. He jerked at unexpected noises, fretted when his mom lit a scented candle, and did not like to go outside.

"Some babies are more difficult than others," Matthew's pediatrician explained.

"Colic," Great-Grandma diagnosed.

"Got your hands full," childless Uncle Ed shook his head.

Matthew's parents, Jeff and Amy, admittedly had between them only limited experience with babies, but they felt in their hearts—suspected and feared—something simply wasn't right with their child. Perhaps Matthew had a physical problem, a condition that could be treated. Neither of them had expected to parent a perfect baby; they knew that all children go through moody spells now and then, but the two of them struggled with the discouragement and exhaustion that came from trying unsuccessfully to comfort their miserable little boy.

Months passed and Matthew grew into a strong and healthy toddler. His hearing checked out perfectly and he did not need glasses. He talked and walked on time and he successfully drank from a cup way before his cousin Michael did.

Jeff and Amy were thankful for their child's healthy body and they took joy in his on-time meeting of developmental milestones. But their joy was repeatedly tested by his deplorable behavior. Matthew flew into rages at the grocery store, at the bank, and at Sunday School. He still slept poorly and had trouble adapting to change. Something as small as a lump in his oatmeal or a new pair of socks with seams that didn't feel right would precipitate a whole morning's worth of tears.

Amy had wanted to, needed to return to part-time work when Matthew turned three years old. But her employment plan did not work out. In less than six months, Matthew was terminated—a nice word for "kicked out"—of a record breaking four different day-care centers because of fighting with other children.

Jeff and Amy tried everything. They talked to him, bribed him, and punished him. They tried to shame him, motivate him, and inspire him into more sociably acceptable behavior.

"Daddy," his mother would ask at the breakfast table each morning, "do you fight with your friends?"

"No!" Jeff would shake his head. "I never fight with my friends."

"Mommy," his daddy would ask," do you fight with your friends?"

"Oh no-ooo," Amy would answer. "I play nice with my friends. I don't hit them and I don't bite them."

"Matthew," Daddy would then ask, "are you going to hit your friends today?"

"NO-OOO!" Matthew would answer with righteous indignation.

"Are you going to play nice today?" Amy would ask.

"Yes!" he would answer with enthusiasm.

And so his mother would take him to the day-care center, would help him out of his coat, and would lead him to the block table or the art center. He would kiss her good-bye and quickly become so engrossed in play that he would hardly notice when she left him. She would ease out of the center, buckle her seatbelt, start her car's engine and think, pray, hope, that maybe, just maybe, Matthew will be good today.

But when Amy would arrive to pick her son up, over and over, afternoon after afternoon, she would be greeted by a grim-faced worker and told once again that Matthew had hit, kicked, or even bitten his playmates.

It wasn't that Matthew misbehaved all the time. On good days, he cuddled in Amy's lap, played ball with Jeff, and colored pictures for Grandma. Some nights he slept all night, woke, dressed, and ate breakfast without a whimper. An alert, intelligent little boy, Matthew easily learned his colors and his letters and even how to count to ten in Spanish.

Matthew's parents loved him more than anything. They would not give up. When the family enjoyed one of Matthew's good days, they thought that life couldn't get any better.

But on those bad days . . .

Matthew was five years old when his mother heard about another child with problems similar to his. It turned out the child suffered from severe food allergies and that once they were treated, his behavior improved.

"I don't think allergies are Matthew's problem," his pediatrician was doubtful, "but I'll make the referral if you really want to look into it."

Jeff and Amy believed it was worth a try.

After taking a lengthy history and examining Matthew, the allergist, Dr. Stone, recommended testing. Matthew would be brought to the clinic prior to breakfast. He would be injected with specific substances and his reactions observed to see if allergic responses were provoked. Did Jeff and Amy understand? Did they wish to proceed?

They did.

And so, two mornings later, Jeff, Amy, and Matthew were ushered into a cheerful playroom set up inside the allergy clinic. Dr. Stone would direct the testing and observe the three of them through a one-way mirror. Matthew, though hungry, was behaving well this morning. He walked around the room, played with some toys, and was compliant when given crayons and art paper and asked to draw some pictures. Within minutes, he was so engrossed in his drawing that he was only momentarily disturbed when a nurse, using a tiny, almost painless needle, gave him an injection. For a moment, he kept on drawing.

Then suddenly, like someone had flipped a switch, Matthew began to wail, to scream, to kick, and to hit. He pounded his fist on the table and turned his chair over. He took a black crayon and a purple one and scribbled all over his careful drawing. Nothing Jeff or Amy did comforted him. He pushed them away and spoke ugly words to them.

Two nurses hurried back into the room. One restrained squirming, screaming Matthew in her arms while the other gave him a second injection, an antidote to the first one. Within seconds he became still. She released her hold and Matthew stood up. He calmly walked over to the table and looked at his drawing, the one he'd scribbled over.

"Who messed up my picture?" He was indignant.

"Somebody turned my chair over." He set the chair back up.

"When do I get to eat?"

❧ ❧

With sparkly brown eyes, curly, sand-colored hair, and a toothy grin planted in the center of a mischievous face, ten-year-old Matthew was a charming kid. Like many boys his age, he tended to be a bit hyperactive and impulsive, but his fun-loving nature and good manners made him, among my son's friends, one of my favorites.

It was not until Russell asked if Matthew could spend the night that I learned of his friend's allergies to common food additives. Such severe allergies as his, his mother Amy told me, are rare. Though avoiding foods containing artificial colors and flavors and those made with preservatives—the foods Matthew reacted to severely—was difficult and sometimes inconvenient, she and his dad did whatever was necessary to provide alternatives for their son.

And Matthew, for the most part, cooperated with his restricted eating. But since once an allergic reaction was over, he seemed to retain little memory of it, he did not comprehend what the fuss was all about. Every so often, he would sneak around and eat something he shouldn't. The last time Matthew pulled such a stunt, Amy told me with a shudder, he secretly bought and ate a whole bag of fruit chews—about the worst thing he could have picked, for the candies were full of artificial colorings and flavorings. Matthew had behaved like a wild man for more than 24 hours after scarfing down the forbidden treats.

So while Amy was pleased when Russell invited Matthew to spend the night, she was a bit apprehensive as well. "I'll bring over his sleeping bag and pajamas and plenty of the foods he can eat so you won't have to worry about it," she told me.

There was no need for her to do that. I didn't want Matthew to feel different, to watch us enjoy something he couldn't have. "Just tell me what Matthew can and can't have," I assured her. "I'll make the same meals for us. It won't be a problem. I promise."

And so she did. And it wasn't a problem. For dinner I made a pot roast and mashed potatoes and offered fruit for dessert. The next morning for breakfast I served made-from-scratch biscuits and country-style gravy. Fresh orange juice and milk completed an easily prepared hot meal.

Russell chewed a breakfast biscuit. "Matthew, what happens to you if eat something you're not supposed to have?"

"Yeah, Matthew," Rachel asked, absently stirring the gravy, "will it make you die or something?"

"Well . . . " Matthew began.

Seeking to head this conversation off, I interrupted. "When Matthew eats something he shouldn't, he doesn't feel good. Certain foods make him feel bad. Make him sort of sick. Pass the juice please."

But Matthew interrupted me. "Oh no, Miz Smith. It's not like that at all. When I eat something I'm not supposed to, I don't feel bad. I feel good! I feel bright and shiny!"

Bright and shiny. That's how Matthew felt?

Not sick. Not cranky. Not bad at all.

Bright and shiny.

I struggled not to smile.

Though I didn't do it, wouldn't dream of doing it, my secret thought was forget the healthy foods, pass this kid some fruit chews!

Light will shine on your ways.
JOB 22:28

CHAPTER THIRTY-FIVE

Lima Beans and Ice Cream

Abby did not like lima beans. Did not believe she could eat them without gagging. Crossed her arms over her chest and decided that this time she was not going to eat them.

None of them.

Not one.

"No ice cream until you eat those beans, young lady," Mama challenged. "I mean it."

Five-year-old Abby, snugly sandwiched between Mama and Grandpa, perched atop the Sears Fall and Winter and Spring and Summer Catalogues, fiddled with her fork, stirred her mashed potatoes, and took a tiny bite of her roll. She did not speak, knew better than to talk back to her mother, but stuck out her lip, kicked at a table leg and gave Grandpa a miserable, long-faced look.

He did not return the gloomy expression. After glancing over Abby's head at her mama, he shot his granddaughter a conspiratorial wink.

Suddenly, Grandpa had Abby's attention. Fork poised in mid-air, she sat up straighter, stopped kicking the table, and followed his gaze to her mother. Mama and Grandma were at this moment engrossed in conversation, talking about some old chicken recipe or blouse pattern or rose bush or something.

Grandpa put his fingers to his lips, then nonchalantly placed his big bony hand on the table next to Abby's plate. Just sort of rested it there for a while. Like it was tired.

Then, not moving his eyes from the faces of Abby's mama and grandma, still managing to appropriately nod and voice his agreement every so often, Grandpa slowly and stealthily inched that hand closer and closer to Abby's plate. Nearer and nearer, closer and closer his fingers moved, first to the edge of Abby's plate, and then, right into her plate. Finally, still watching Abby's mama and Grandma (for you never knew about those two women; they could be sneaky), his thumb and forefinger touched and groped until they found a big old fat lima bean.

Quick as a flash, he picked that lima bean up off Abby's plate and popped it into his mouth.

Abby covered her mouth with her hand to keep from giggling, but Grandpa's face never changed.

Abby watched, and when she was sure her mama wasn't looking, she helped Grandpa out by sliding the lima beans off the edge of her plate. Trying not to actually touch the beans, Abby used her knife to push them Grandpa's direction. That way he could get to the nasty vegetables easier; his hand wouldn't have to hunt so hard.

Their system worked. Moments later, Mama looked Abby's way and was pleased as could be to see that she had eaten every one of her lima beans. Mama was so proud she even gave Abby an extra scoop of ice cream.

Grandpa got two scoops too.

Grandpa was a farmer by trade. Nothing pleased him more than planting seeds in the ground and watching them grow into tall green plants. He was good at it. Most folks did their planting by the Farmer's Almanac or by which phase the moon happened to be in. Not Grandpa. Although he did take both into account, Grandpa planted when he felt in his bones the time was right. Didn't matter what any of the neighbors did.

Grandpa's crops always came in good.

Only once in his life did Grandpa try another line of permanent work. Like he did every winter when there was no farming to be done, rather than sitting around whittling and dreaming of spring, Grandpa got a town job. Usually he found work as a carpenter because he was good at building things as well as growing them. But this particular season, instead of carpentering, Grandpa went to work at a warehouse that packed, crated, and shipped already manufactured nuts and bolts.

An indoor job.

The first one he'd ever had.

"Ruby," he said after his first week, "I may just keep this job. Not even go back to farming. Pay's good. I'm in out of the weather. When it rains I don't get wet. When it's cold I stay warm. When it gets hot this summer, I'll have me a place to work in the shade. Don't know how a feller could beat a job like this."

It was a good job.

The place where Grandpa worked was not exactly in town. Just close to it. In fact, it was situated, oddly, in the middle of a farmer's winter-barren field. The building that housed the nuts and bolts was a long narrow one with four tiny windows cut high up in the end walls.

During the winter, when the sky stayed mostly gray, when it was nice to work inside where it was warm, Grandpa hardly noticed those windows. But as the days lengthened and the air began to clear, Grandpa kept spending more and more time looking out those openings to the sky.

One night, after Grandma's fried chicken supper, Grandpa reminded her, "Ruby, a man would have to be crazy to quit a job this good to go back to farming. As it stands, I don't have to worry about no drought or grasshoppers or wore out tools or nothing. Just show up every day and get a nice paycheck at the end of the week. I am one lucky man to have a job like this."

When the sun began to shine more days than not, Grandpa took to eating his lunch and taking his break in front of those windows. Every day he'd drag a crate to the end of the building and climb up on it so he could get at better look at the outside. He'd stand there and eat his sandwich, munch on his cookies, and drink his tea. Never one to keep important information to himself, Grandpa helpfully gave the other men twice daily weather reports.

"Looks like sunshine."

"Big old thunderstorm coming up."

"No wind today. Not a bit."

"Ruby," he said before bed, "I've got the best job a man could have. The work's not hard on me but I have plenty to keep me busy."

By the time March rolled around, Grandpa was eating his lunch and taking his break outside.

"It's a good job, Ruby. A real good job."

But on the early spring day that the landowner took a plow to that field, the day Grandpa stuck his head out the window and caught his first whiff of that rich, black, just-turned-over-soil, he could stand it no more. For as far as any farmer is concerned, there is no sweeter smell on earth than fresh dirt. That day, Grandpa took off his work gloves, laid down his tools, and told the boss that he was sorry, but he had to go.

There was planting to be done.

Much obliged.

Hoped the man would keep him in mind for a job next winter.

"Ruby," he told her when he got home, "God did not make a man to spend all his days in the shade."

❧ ❧

Abby and I lived next door to each other when my husband and I were first married. She and I had a lot in common. We both liked to read, to sew, and to make bread from scratch. Most importantly, neither of us could stomach lima beans, and we both loved ice cream.

From Abby, I learned to sew a French seam.

From me, Abby gleaned a recipe for Honey Whole Wheat Loaves.

From Abby, I received a book by my now-favorite author.

Unlike me, Abby loved to work in the dirt. (I was content to buy flowers from the florist and strawberries from the supermarket.)

Abby lived for the arrival of her seed catalogues and the day that the danger of a frost was considered well-passed. Abby could tame a trailing vine, knew just where and when to prune a rose bush, and got more excited about compost than I thought any woman should.

I did not share her outdoor enthusiasm, and in fact missed our time together in the house.

"What's the big deal about gardening?" I whined from my porch. "Let's bake some bread, make a trip to the bookstore, check out the fabric sale. Anything to get you out of that dirt. Come on. Please?"

Abby, up to her elbows in earth and grinning like she was in heaven, reared back on her heels, shoved her hair out of her eyes, and threw me an extra pair of gardening gloves she had in her overall pocket.

"Forget it. Get down here and help me. Don't you know that God did not make a woman to spend all her days in the shade?"

I didn't.

But I do now.

Maybe the seed catalogue I ordered will be in the mail today.

My eyes will watch over them for their good,
and I will bring them back to this land.
JEREMIAH 24:6

CHAPTER THIRTY-SIX

White Bread

*N*either my husband nor I are good at managing money. It seems that in our household we almost always run out of money before we run out of month. We are able to pay our bills, and our family has everything it truly needs, but sometimes both of us get a bit uneasy at the end-of-the-month depth to which our checking account dips.

For some reason, the frugality that should run in both our genes somehow seems to have skipped us. For, while because of our careless spending habits we have trouble making ends meet on a middle-class budget, both of our penny-pinching grandparents survived and raised families during The Great Depression.

Randy's grandparents on his mother's side lived in town. Like most all her neighbors, his grandmother stayed home and kept house. His grandfather either caught a ride or walked the several miles to a box factory job where he put in as many hours as were allotted to him. The family did not own a car and they felt lucky to rent a few rooms from a recently widowed, childless woman.

My mother-in-law, Dorothy, was their only child. She re-
members, during those lean years, consuming meal after meal
of boiled potatoes topped with a weak-sounding concoction
her parents called water gravy. Though they did purchase
some milk, it was so expensive all that was bought was ear-
marked for small-framed daughter Dorothy to drink with her
breakfast.

On the other hand, my grandparents, whom I called
Grandma and Pop, were country people. For food they raised
a garden, chickens, and a hog. During the depression, to
make even a little bit of money the two of them picked both
corn and cotton for other folks.

Grandma tells of leaving her babies—my dad Louie and
his older sister Joy—on a quilt under a tree while she picked
cotton. Many times, at about the middle of a row, she would
hear them begin to cry. Though she would look up and worry
and wonder if her children cried because they were hungry or
hot or because they'd been snake or spider-bit, Grandma
knew she couldn't stop her picking. So she would just lower
her head and pluck the cotton as fast as she could in order to
finish one row and make it back down the next one to check
on them.

At one point during the worst of those times, Pop and five
other men traveled across the state, hoping to find work. The
six of them crowded into one old car, money for gas and a few
days food pooled between them. Once they'd reached where
they were going, the men inquired around town about any
work to be had. They were all disappointed to find instead of
the long-term, good-paying factory jobs they'd hoped for, just
a few weeks worth of meager field labor.

But they took those weeks of work. The hours they toiled
in the fields were long and the conditions miserable. Stout
young men that they were, they still found it difficult to
stand up to such labor on the sparse food they rationed for

themselves. Lacking a place to stay, they had brought quilts and had planned to sleep on the ground next to the field. But because the land was infested with rattlesnakes, they were forced to sleep—all weary unwashed six of them—crammed shoulder to shoulder in the seats of the car.

On my bedroom dresser sits a framed photo of my grandparents. They were just a young couple when the photo was taken. Grandma and Pop stand next to each other, but they do not touch. Their faces carry hard, pinched looks. My grandfather, a man in his twenties, responsible for feeding a wife and two babies, looks frightened and angry.

I imagine he was.

❦ ❦

During the depression, white flour became both scarce and expensive, especially in the rural South. Instead of offering up soft, yeast-risen loaves of light bread or baskets of fluffy, white, baking powder biscuits, resourceful southern housewives served their families endless cakes of yellow, oven-baked cornbread. Though the coarse and crumbly substitute proved filling and tasty enough (moistened with the juice of cooked vegetables or crumbled into a glass of tangy buttermilk, cornbread is really pretty good eating), Southern folks remembered and sorely missed their beloved white bread. And they rejoiced when hard times eased and it appeared back on their tables.

Those lean, cornbread-eating years and the more prosperous ones that followed spawned a curious, back-woods, southern phrase: "You are eating white bread now!" These are the words some folks, even today, offer as a fitting commentary, an acknowledgement of a blessing, upon any exceptionally good thing that might come a person's way.

My great-aunt spoke of white bread to me on my wedding day and again on the day I gave birth to my first child. I've heard "you are eating white bread now" spoken to the new owners of a white-shuttered house and "he's sure 'nuff eating white bread today" uttered through proud, hot tears when an oldest grandson graduated from medical school.

And while personally I like grainy, whole wheat bread much better than white bread, and though I myself think there is nothing better than a buttered cornbread muffin, I am only a generation gone from the hard-working people who coined the phrase. And so, I often catch myself musing, when life is going especially well, girl, you are eating white bread now!

And I am.

There are times when the daily bread—be it white, whole wheat, or corn—that makes up each of our lives becomes so full, so busy, that we just know we can't cram any more in. Instead of enjoying the feast, we eat on the run. And when we are hurriedly gobbling up such big bites out of life, failing to sit down and savor, not taking time to touch or to taste, we are missing the sweetness that is slathered on the cut side of each new day. Life, at such a pace, becomes dry and stale instead of rich and full of goodness.

My feisty, now gone-to-glory friend Sidney, confronted me at such a time with yet more words about bread: "Don't be so afraid!" she said impatiently. "Let go! Cast your bread upon the waters. I tried it and mine came back buttered!"

Thankfully, I heard, really heard, Sidney's words. I began to try and slow down. I learned to let go, to trust God, and take life as it comes. I'm not there yet, but today I am learning to savor lots of moments and to sometimes squander whole hours. I seek to see the joy in the simple, to catch the heavenly that is in the earthly, to uncover the light in the dark, and to discover the extraordinary in the ordinary.

And I almost always find it.

If my friend Sidney was still alive, I would tell her that she was right. My bread, the bread of my life, has come back to

me, over and over again, not just buttered, but dripping with
a taste that is even sweeter than honey.

May yours do the same.

It is my father who gives you the true bread from heaven.
JOHN 6:32

About the Author

ANNETTE SMITH authored the bestselling collection of stories *Whispers of Angels* (more than 40,000 in print). A longtime home-healthcare nurse, she currently works as a writer and camp nurse at a wilderness program for troubled teens. She lives in Texas with her husband, Randy, and their two teenagers.

Other Books by
Annette Smith

❧ ❦

Whispers of Angels

Throughout her nursing career, Annette Smith has witnessed tender moments of caring and compassion, despair and doubt, love and laughter. *Whispers of Angels* is a heartwarming collection of "good medicine" that will bring you smiles of joy and a renewed perspective on life. Finding a good dose of humor and glimpses of the divine in hospital rooms and doctors' offices, Annette Smith reminds you that life is a journey to be celebrated, and that in someone else's story you will find echoes of your own.

Help! My Little Girl's Growing Up

Throughout her nursing career, Annette Smith has witnessed tender moments of caring and compassion, despair and doubt, love and laughter. *Whispers of Angels* is a heartwarming collection of "good medicine" that will bring you smiles of joy and a renewed perspective on life. Finding a good dose of humor and glimpses of the divine in hospital rooms and doctors' offices, Annette Smith reminds you that life is a journey to be celebrated, and that in someone else's story you will find echoes of your own.

❦ ❧

Where Roots Grow Deep
Bob Welch

From the acclaimed author of *A Father for All Seasons* comes a collection of heartwarming stories about families and the importance of leaving a legacy of love for generations yet to come. In *Where Roots Grow Deep,* Bob Welch offers memorable and moving true stories written with humor and rich insight. Using the timeless analogy of nurturing and growing trees, Bob points to how critical it is to leave a legacy of love for our children and for generations to come. It's never too late, he writes, to begin creating that legacy. "The best time to plant a tree was 20 years ago. The second-best time is now."

Beyond the Picket Fence
Lori Wick

Bestselling author Lori Wick brings her vibrant faith and romantic heart to this delightful collection of stories about camping in the wilds, celebrating Christmas, finding "first" love, and more. These enchanting and lively snapshots of faith will capture your heart.

A Father for All Seasons
Bob Welch

This highly personal book gives encouragement to dads and sons by reiterating an important message: Fathers need sons, sons need fathers, and the world is a better place when the two connect. Excerpts of this book have appeared in *Focus on the Family* and *Reader's Digest* magazines.